The Social
Work Portfolio

The Social Work Portfolio

A Student's Guide
to Evidencing Your Practice

Lee-Ann Fenge
Kate Howe
Mel Hughes
Gill Calvin Thomas

McGraw Hill Education Open University Press

Open University Press
McGraw-Hill Education
McGraw-Hill House
Shoppenhangers Road
Maidenhead
Berkshire
England
SL6 2QL

email: enquiries@openup.co.uk
world wide web: www.openup.co.uk

and Two Penn Plaza, New York, NY 10121-2289, USA

First published 2014

Copyright © Lee-Ann Fenge, Kate Howe, Mel Hughes, Gill Calvin Thomas, 2014

A catalogue record of this book is available from the British Library

ISBN-13: 978-0-335-24531-4
ISBN-10: 0-335-24531-5
eISBN: 978-0-335-24532-1

Library of Congress Cataloging-in-Publication Data
CIP data applied for

Typeset by Aptara, Inc.

Contents

The authors

Lee-Ann Fenge

Dr Lee-Ann Fenge is Deputy Director of the National Centre for Post-Qualifying Social Work at Bournemouth University. She has extensive experience of teaching on both undergraduate and postgraduate programmes. Her research and practice interests are with seldom heard groups and older people. She is particularly interested in participatory methodologies and the use of narratives in education, research and practice.

Kate Howe

Kate Howe is a senior lecturer in social work at Bournemouth University. She teaches on both qualifying and post-qualifying social work programmes, and has particular experience in practice learning. More recently her research and practice interests are in working with conflict and developing leadership skills.

Mel Hughes

Dr Mel Hughes is a senior lecturer in social work at Bournemouth University. She leads on practice learning on both the BA and MA qualifying programmes. Her research and teaching interests include educational theory, transformative learning, critical reflection, service user involvement, and the use of narratives in education, research and practice.

Gill Calvin Thomas

Although now retired, Gill was an experienced practice teacher and senior lecturer within the Centre of Social Work and Social Policy at Bournemouth University. Her social work career spanned many decades, working in a variety of settings in adult care. She became a training officer in a local authority with a keen interest in equal opportunities in the workplace. While at Bournemouth University Gill's academic and research interests lay particularly in the promotion of student learning in practice, which included research into the experiences of students from diverse backgrounds and the rich learning that could be gained by students working in partnership with service users.

List of tables and figures

Tables

Figures

Preface

This book is aimed primarily at undergraduate social work students. Students often have questions about the purpose of the portfolio, and how to effectively evidence their practice learning within the portfolio. This text is structured in a way to guide your learning in placement, and to explore the best ways of evidencing your learning within the portfolio format. As we developed this book, key changes have occurred in social work education and practice as a result of the Social Work Reform Board. The Professional Capabilities Framework (PCF) proposed by the Social Work Reform Board (2010b), and proposals by Munro (2011), support the paradigm shift from technical rationality – that is, learning and applying a set of fixed rules – to one which acknowledges and legitimizes the role of reflective practice. The text is therefore mindful of these changes, and sets the use of the portfolio within the PCF, exploring the use of the portfolio in your qualifying programme, and beyond.

The portfolio is a key part of the summative assessment within qualifying social work programmes, and is a key indicator of a student's ability to practice. All students completing a qualifying programme in social work are required to complete a practice portfolio to provide evidence of their learning in practice. This will include linking theory to practice, demonstrating key professional values as well as demonstrating how they map onto the PCF. A key element drawing these strands together is the ability of students to demonstrate an ability to critically reflect upon their practice. The portfolio as a device enables students to demonstrate their learning in terms of developing core knowledge, values and skills.

The book is divided into eight chapters. Each chapter uses a range of reflective activities, practice educator comments, and student testimony to illustrate the discussion.

Chapter 1 gets to grips with what a portfolio is, and how to make best use of it in your learning journey. It considers the different definitions and purposes of portfolios, and explores how to prepare and plan your portfolio.

Chapter 2 considers how to evidence your capability using the Professional Capabilities Framework for social workers. It considers what 'good' evidence is when using the nine professional capabilities within your portfolio.

Chapter 3 supports you to reflect upon your own learning needs and learning style. It provides a range of activities to help you make sense of yourself as a learner, and to reflect upon both academic learning and experiential learning from the workplace.

Chapter 4 explores working with your practice educator in terms of practice learning and portfolio development. Exercises and activities to support good supervision with your practice educator are explored.

Chapter 5 explores how you can evidence the use of theory in your portfolio. It considers the links between theory and practice, and includes a range of tools and activities to support you in demonstrating this within your practice and your portfolio.

Chapter 6 explores the use of 'self' within your portfolio. You will be encouraged to develop a reflective and academic style in your written work to enable you to appropriately evidence your personal and professional development within the portfolio.

Chapter 7 discusses the importance of evidencing meaningful service user and carer involvement within your placement and portfolio.

Chapter 8 concludes the book by exploring how your portfolio can be used as a basis for future continuing professional development and learning, including the need to develop personal development plans and the role of the Assessed and Supported Year in Employment (AYSE).

We feel that these chapters will help you make the most of your portfolio, and enable you to consider the best evidence to demonstrate your professional learning within it.

Acknowledgements

We are grateful to a number of social work students, practice educators and service users who have offered their perspectives on student placements and portfolio development throughout this book. We have listed them below.

Chapter 3

Ann Daniel	Practice educator
Georgina Brown	Social work student

Chapter 4

Ann Bowler	Service user
Dorinda Howard	Student
Lisa Hoyle	Practice educator
Lucy Reavenall	Student
June Sadd	Service user and experienced practice educator

Chapter 5

Claire Lawrence	Student
Dr Francisca Veale	Practice educator

Chapter 7

Ann Bowler	Service user
Paul Danto	Placement supervisor
Dorinda Howard	Student
Memory Majome	Student
Kirsty Pybus	Practice educator

Chapter 8

Ann Daniel	Practice educator
Matt Taylor	Social work manager and professional doctorate student

1 Getting started

Kate Howe

Introduction

'Why a portfolio?' is a question (or a moan) posed by many students, particularly when the purpose and structure are not clear. It is sometimes followed up with statements such as:

> 'It's easier to just write an essay.'
> 'Can't I just get the practice educator to write a report? S/he knows what I am capable of.'
> 'It's hard enough doing the work, let alone having to put together a portfolio.'

The aim of this chapter is to explore the reasons for portfolios being a feature of social work education, and to help you to understand the importance of creating what can be one of the most significant (and satisfying) pieces of work that you will complete during your social work qualifying programme.

The chapter starts by considering the different definitions and purposes of portfolios. It then continues with looking at how you can prepare and plan to complete your portfolio. As portfolios are different from essays, and shorter pieces of assessment, you might need new work strategies to be successful. This chapter therefore explores how to make the process as easy and enjoyable as possible, and includes activities to help guide you.

By the end of the chapter you will:

- Know the purpose of your portfolio.
- Know what you need to do to complete a successful portfolio.
- Be able to create a plan of how you will complete your portfolio.

What is a portfolio?

Portfolios can be described in many ways. They are usually a collection of documents or work with some common thread that draws them together. Short definitions, such as the ones below, can be useful in developing an initial understanding. They have been referred to as:

- 'a professional scrapbook' (Byrne et al. 2009)
- 'a compendium of materials that document accomplishments' (Swigonski et al. 2006)
- 'a complete and permanent record of progress during a period of study' (Rhodes and Tallantyre in Taylor et al. 1999)

Timmins' (2008: 2) definition is particularly applicable to our discussion of portfolios in relation to social work students: 'A portfolio is a collection and cohesive account of work-based learning that contains relevant evidence from practice and critical reflection on this evidence. Portfolios have been used in education for some time now, and particularly on professional programmes.'

The contents of a portfolio and how it is presented can be just as diverse as the definitions. The traditional picture is of a ring binder of documents that meet the specifications of the programme. This can include learning agreements, critical reflections of observations, analyses of practice, summaries of work, supervision records, etc. Some programmes will be very specific and rigid about what to include, in what becomes a minimal portfolio. Others will be less selective and expect a student to incorporate most of the work completed in placement into a more weighty folder. More recently e-portfolios have been used; these can sometimes give added flexibility to what evidence can be included, and provide the opportunity to update and reorganize in a more flexible way.

All of these have pros and cons for the student. However, the key advice is to know the requirements of your particular programme and follow that rigorously. Many of the complaints about portfolios from readers and assessors stem from students including documents that they deem are important, but are not required, or leaving out documents that are essential to the evaluation.

Key point

Portfolios have a multitude of definitions, and social work programmes will differ in their interpretation and requirements. It is imperative that you know what the requirements of your social work programme are. Most programmes will provide guidance, usually through a handbook. Take time to read it to know what it is that you need to do. At an early stage the detail may not be clear, but you can get an overview, and start to know what questions to ask

What is the purpose of a portfolio?

Before going any further, it is worth noting that some hold a very cynical and negative perspective about portfolios: that they are some kind of exercise in making the student work hard in pointless tasks. A well-constructed portfolio compiled by a motivated student will not be like this, so let's look at what are some of the more positive and enlightening reasons for using portfolios in practice learning.

Assessment and evaluation

Assessing your capability to become a qualified social worker or progress to the next stage is probably the most obvious purpose of a portfolio. A portfolio contains evidence or information that is used by others to determine whether you have acquired the knowledge, skills and values required to reach the next level of your social work development. The portfolio brings together samples of your practice work that best demonstrate your achievements.

As they often contain multiple samples of work, they enable you to provide a more in-depth and authentic representation of your achievements.

The advantage of producing a portfolio is that it allows for individual differences to be considered, while still being a method of assessment that is reliable, valid and consistent.

Social work programmes need to take account of:

- the diversity of opportunities available for students in different placements
- the different skills, knowledge and learning needs of individual students.

Social work has a long tradition of celebrating diversity and portfolios are a good vehicle to accommodate the uniqueness of your developing practice in your particular placement.

Assessment is often divided into *summative* and *formative* processes.

Summative assessment is usually at the end of the placement where the portfolio provides the evidence that you have reached the standard required for that stage of your development. This will usually be linked to the Professional Capabilities Framework (for more detail see Chapter 2), but could also have other programme-specific outcomes that are being assessed. The assessment is often carried out by practice educators and lecturers linked to your programme, who will read portfolios, and then attend a practice assessment panel where the final decision is made. When looking at the weaknesses of this system it is easy to see that there are many different individuals involved in this process, and therefore the possibility of different opinions can lead to some inconsistency of decisions. In my experience the decision on the majority of portfolios is unanimous and uncontroversial, as the standards have clearly been met. The difficult decisions are about portfolios that are borderline in meeting the requirements, and this is where disputes can occur. As this is inherent in the system the best way to manage it is to make sure your portfolio **clearly** meets the standards required.

Formative assessment is the ongoing feedback about your development throughout your placement. You may have a programme where you prepare an interim or midway portfolio where an independent practice educator or lecturer will give feedback and suggestions for progress in the next part of the placement. In addition, your practice educator, through supervision, observations and written feedback will be providing you with lots of 'formative assessment' comments that can help you to judge your progress and also make any changes necessary to reach the final goal of passing the summative assessment.

Key point

Be clear about the assessment processes for your programme.
Be clear about the assessment criteria: What does your portfolio need to evidence to ensure you clearly meet the standards set?

Promoting student learning

Another and equally important purpose for a portfolio is that it provides a vehicle for learning and development. This is summed up in the following quotation:

A portfolio is a purposeful collection of work that exhibits the learner's efforts, progress and achievements. In the course of learning the portfolio becomes a kind of autobiography of growth. By learning to organize their learning experiences for themselves, and sharing them with others, they were able to get a deeper understanding of themselves. The portfolio helps the learner extract meaning from the experience by analytic reflection. It will increase the students' involvement in, responsibility for and ownership of his/her learning. (Jarvinen and Kohenen 1995, cited in Taylor et al. 1999: 149)

Activity 1.1: Reflection point

What do you think are some of the key aspects of this definition?

The idea of an autobiography of growth represents the best intentions of portfolios; they should be something personal and unique to your experience in this period of time, and recognize the learning that will be taking place in the good and not so good times.

This definition also highlights the sense of ownership a student should feel for their portfolio. It is not only your responsibility, but also your creation, and so is something that you can take pride in.

The authors also look at reflection as being a key tool in developing a meaningful portfolio that represents progress and achievements and, as such, has a dynamic place in practice learning, where ongoing development is valued and explored.

Key point

A portfolio has two main purposes:

1 As a tool for learning about social work practice and your own development.
2 As an assessment instrument to evaluate whether you have reached the required standard to move to the next stage of social work education.

Seven reasons for portfolios being purposeful

We can break this down a little further by adapting Courts and McInerney's (1993, in Swigonski et al. 2006) list of ways portfolios can be used to support personal reflection, instruction, and assessment, to understand what you might be able to achieve through completing a portfolio.

1 **To provide an opportunity to reflect on your own performance**
   As we have said already, most portfolios will have some elements that want you to reflect on your practice. Social work programmes demand that you develop the skill of reflection as a method of demonstrating professional capability. If this is your first placement then the idea of writing about your own practice, linking it to theory and developing a critical awareness, can be quite daunting. Chapter 5 will help you to start developing this skill, and other chapters will encourage you to reflect on specific areas of your learning.
2 **To encourage you to choose for yourself what is or is not important in your performance**
   Learning to select what is important is a core skill in social work. Most social work portfolios ask for specific items of evidence to be included, rather than including everything.

Therefore throughout your placement you will be deciding what to include in your portfolio. Even the most prescriptive or comprehensive portfolio will require you to leave out information. The ability to make decisions for yourself, based only on the information you have, is an important learning process.

Students often report that this is the most daunting part of the portfolio and want to include everything 'just in case'. Practice being discerning right from the beginning of your placement: a) use the assessment criteria and, b) discuss with your practice educator what criteria to use to judge what good evidence is. You will also find advice in the subsequent chapters of this book that will help you to make those decisions.

3 **To help you to see connections across learning experiences both on placement and in the university**

The difference between compiling a portfolio and a discrete piece of work is that a portfolio allows a learning event to be explored from different perspectives. For instance, the connections between the teaching about attachment, or discrimination, or using questions and how to assess the needs of a service user, will start to make sense. The different tasks needed to complete a portfolio will also embed this process. For example, you may write a critical incident analysis that focuses on a single event. At a different time you may reflect more generally on a different occasion that brings in a wider perspective of the service user situation, the relationship, and your practice. The assessor comments can also help to draw out the links between pieces of work and skills development.

Students report that this can bring about 'light bulb' moments, when suddenly the relevance of many different pieces of learning fit together like the completion of a jigsaw puzzle. Learning logs or reflective journals can also help to encourage this, and can be included as evidence in some portfolios.

4 **To provide a concrete basis for open, learner-centred discussions between you and your practice educator/placement supervisor/tutor to explore what is being learned**

Sharing the learning through the different tasks involved in a portfolio can enable both the student and the practice educator to recognize themes that can be developed through supervision discussions. Specific write-ups, whether through reflective logs or critical incident analyses about a particular piece of work or service user, will give you the opportunity to think on your own and in your own time. Supervision discussions, before and/or after, will add another dimension and depth to your learning. Connections between different pieces of work will also add to your learning. It can also help to decide what is needed to consider the focus of future work.

5 **To recognize that learning is a cumulative process**

A portfolio can be used to show the development of skills and abilities over a period of time. It is therefore acceptable for a portfolio to include pieces of work from early in placement that are not 'as good' as later work. Many students have commented that looking back over a portfolio is a valuable experience in appreciating the progress they have made. A portfolio – or parts of it – can be brought into supervision sessions to review, and used to recognize what and how learning is happening.

6 **To identify areas of strength and weakness, and to plan ways to optimize strengths and work on the weaker points**

As you are completing your portfolio, and in discussions with your practice educators and tutors, you will become aware of where you feel strongest and what areas need attention. You may be asked to make this assessment for yourself, and this is part of identifying and taking some responsibility for your own learning. Many placements have a midway review, and the record of this discussion can direct the focus of learning for the next period of practice.

Assessment reports from the practice educator will also provide a summative assessment of your achievement during the placement, as well as identifying what your learning and development needs are in the future.

7   **To provide a concrete, conscious sense of your accomplishments and growth**
This might seem to be difficult to contemplate at the start of a placement, but many of the comments from students after handing in their portfolios say how positive they feel about their achievement.

A student perspective

'I am rather proud of my portfolio and what I did on placement, and I don't mind sharing it with other professionals in the future.'

'It was satisfying to see all my hard work come together into something I am proud of.'

Activity 1.2: Purpose of your portfolio

Spend a few minutes thinking about the different purposes of your portfolio and which ones you feel are most important. You may also have thought of others.

Write them down – maybe in your journal or placement log – so that you can return to it when you are completing your portfolio. It may help you to keep focused.

Key point

- This is **your** portfolio.
- **You** are responsible for what goes into it and how it looks.
- Your portfolio communicates a representation of you to the outside world. Make sure your portfolio gives the message about you that you want to portray.

Preparing yourself: the power of positive thinking

Portfolios are important and take time to complete. It is important to get into the right frame of mind to take on this task confidently. Take some time to complete the following activity: it will help you develop a clear, constructive and positive attitude to your portfolio.

Activity 1.3: Visualizing success

Imagine yourself reading your portfolio about a month after your placement has finished and being able to make comments like the students
quoted in the last section. Hear yourself saying 'I am proud of my portfolio' as you hand it in to be assessed. How does that feel? Being able to
visualize yourself creating a good portfolio is a great motivator to getting
on with the task.

So let's take this a little further:

1 What do **you** want to achieve from this portfolio task?
This needs to be a positive statement. For example: 'I want to make
sure I don't fail' is a negative statement. 'I want to get through' or
'finish' is also not very positive. You might think about using words
such as 'increasing', 'improving', 'completing', 'proving'. An example of
a positive statement could be: 'I will produce a portfolio that meets all
the requirements to my highest standard.'

Make it as specific as possible: phrases such as 'I want to pass'
or 'I want to succeed' are very general. The more detail you can provide, and that you can own, about what you want to achieve, the more
motivated to succeed you will be.

Think about what **you** want and write down your statement. You
might include the skills or knowledge you want to achieve and demonstrate in the portfolio (for example, the ability to integrate theory and
practice). You might include something about the process of completing
the portfolio (for example, that you will work on the portfolio steadily
throughout the placement).

2 How will you know you have achieved your outcome?
What will be your evidence?

What will you see? Maybe your completed portfolio with a really
positive assessment feedback.

What will you hear? Maybe your practice educator praising how well
you have completed the portfolio, how well you have demonstrated the
skills you wanted to develop. Maybe you will tell yourself how well you
have done.

What will you feel? Maybe a glow of pride as you hold the portfolio,
heavy with the work you have done.

Spend a few minutes really imagining that you have successfully
completed your portfolio and achieved your outcome.

3 What are the barriers or obstacles you are likely to encounter?
It is good to think through these questions and take action as soon as
possible.

Who or what might get in the way of your achieving your outcome?
How might you overcome this?

4 What resources (that you control) need to be in place to achieve this
goal?
This is about the resources available to you that are in your control. For
example, you cannot rely on your children going to sleep at six every

evening, but you can commit to getting up an hour earlier in the morning to read or make notes.

You might identify internal resources such as maintaining commitment or motivation, and how you will gain these.

You might also think of other external resources such as an organized work space.

5 Who else is involved?
Is the success of the project entirely your responsibility? You may need to rely on others for support, or to do something; if so, what is it that you need and how can you ensure that you get it?

For example, do you need to set out clear expectations for yourself and others to ensure everyone knows and agrees the plan?

6 Is it worth it? (It is always useful to look at how we might sabotage ourselves.)
Is there anything that will be lost if you achieve your outcome? For example, will your best friend threaten to not see you anymore if you don't go out every Friday?

How will you manage any of these interruptions?

7 Desirability check?
On a scale of 1 to 10, how much are you clear and committed to your outcome? If it is lower than 7, what else do you need to do to make it higher? You may need to revisit some of the questions above to make your outcome more compelling?

8 What is the first step?
This could be to undertake some detailed planning to work out what you need to do and when, and gain some real clarity about the task you have now decided is important to you.

Planning and managing your portfolio

The portfolio and placement may be the longest sustained piece of work you have undertaken so far and is therefore worth taking time to plan. Coleman et al. (2002) state 'Meaningful portfolios are seldom created without a struggle', and so recognizing it as an ongoing project may help to maintain progress.

Step 1: Define the task

This is a crucial step to set firm foundations. The handbook and advice from tutors is critically important here. The following questions can help:

- What exactly do you need to do – what are the course requirements?
- What are the learning outcomes to be evidenced?
- Have you read the handbook?
- Do you understand what is being asked of you? What don't you understand? Who are you going to ask, and when?

> **A practice educator perspective**
>
> My top tip would be that you ensure you are conversant with the hand-book prior to the placement starting so that the precious time in supervision can be saved to discuss the issues and learning in placement.

Think about writing a plan of what you need to complete – task by task. Add comments and questions that occur to you, and take these up with the relevant person when appropriate.

Step 2: Consider the timings

1 **Time planning: What are the critical dates you need to be aware of?**
   List all your commitments relating to the portfolio, your placement, your other work, as well as your personal and social commitments for the duration of the placement. Think about the portfolio as an ongoing project with regular weekly tasks to complete. You can make notes as you go along as memory joggers. One such task might be to learn new terminology as it appears – try to use it in assignments to demonstrate your comprehension of concepts and ideas.

> **A student perspective**
>
> I did it as I went along (which was my goal for the placement), which I think helped as I avoided a last minute panic.

2 **Create a schedule**
   Either find an appropriate piece of paper or create a weekly calendar on your computer, phone or tablet for the duration of the placement.

   * Put in all the set and immoveable dates that you know about.
   * Start to factor in the preparation time and writing time for assignments.
   * Add in other commitments that need time. Be realistic.
   * Add in 'downtime' as an essential part of placement. It is important!
   * Add in review time. This may be just for you, or you might want to include your practice educator or family members to ensure that your schedule is meeting your needs.
   * Identify contingency time so that it will be possible to get back on schedule if unplanned problems get in the way.

3 **Time management**
   A constant complaint from students undertaking practice learning is that there is never enough time to complete the portfolio as well as a full-time placement, and fit in the rest of life. It is tempting to leave the compiling of the portfolio to the last minute. However, the best portfolios are the ones where the student has taken time and care to ensure everything is included in an organized and coherent way.

So let's look at some ideas about time management to see how 'time' can be created. This is an important skill to develop in preparation for being a social worker, so it is worth spending time to develop good strategies now. Please see Table 1.1 which illustrates Covey's (2004) model of Self Management. It offers a way of helping to prioritize where your energy and resources need to be directed. He does not see it as a time management tool, but more about self-management.

The essence of the model is to recognize there are two factors that define any activity: *important* and *urgent*. Urgent activities are there in front of you, pressing you to take action – for example, a ringing phone, or an unexpected visitor wanting to see you. Important activities are the ones that are related to results. Sometimes they are the bigger pieces of work, but these are the activities that will make the difference. We react to urgent matters, but important tasks, particularly if they are not urgent, need proactivity.

Quadrant 1 is the most exhausting place to be, and 'burn out' in social work comes from spending most of your working day there. The consequences to health are obvious, and also the only place anyone wants to go after a long time here is to Quadrant 4 or possibly 3, just to get some downtime.

Quadrant 2 is the most productive use of work time, and is the heart of effective self-management. When you are stressed and not coping it is the important and not urgent work that gets left behind. This is the worst place to 'rob' time from as it can produce more effective ways of working. The aim is to grow the amount of time you spend in Quadrant 2.

Quadrants 3 and 4 are where time can be 'wasted'. Careful analysis of where 'time goes' will often identify these tasks.

Balance: The aim of effective self-management is to spend the majority of your time in Quadrant 2, and reduce time spent in Quadrant 1. Reduction of time in Quadrants 3 and 4 will then release time to be spent in Quadrant 2, and so what is left becomes manageable in the system.

Rebalancing the workload will come from taking time from the activities of Quadrants 3 and 4; as you can see, they are the non-important tasks. It may be difficult to shrink Quadrant 1 initially, but focusing on increasing the quality work of Quadrant 2 should limit the number of urgent demands.

Table 1.1 Self Management Model (Covey, 2004)

	Urgent	Not urgent
High importance	**1 Quadrant of demand** **(Daily reality)** Crisis Pressing problems Deadline projects Critical tasks	**2 Quadrant of quality** Planned time for projects (portfolio) Prevention planning Relationship building New opportunities/projects Self-development Purposeful recreation
Low importance	**3 Quadrant of illusion** Interruptions Some calls and mail Pressing matters without impact Popular activities Activities you feel obliged to do Some meetings	**4 Quadrant of waste (Escape)** Trivia Time wasters Internet surfing Some phone calls Socializing/gossip

(Adapted from Covey 2004)

Activity 1.4: Managing your time well

Using the template below:

1 Look back and either take one day in placement and list all the activities you engaged in during a 24-hour period, or consider all your activities over a few days.
2 Now categorize them into the four quadrants.
3 Estimate how much time you spent in each quadrant.
4 Look carefully at what you might have been able to do differently. Remember that the way to 'grow' time is by reducing the amount of activity in Quadrants 3 and 4.
5 Identify two or three steps you can carry out over a week to balance the system better.
6 After a week, review how well you did.

	Urgent	Not urgent
High importance	**1 Quadrant of demand** (Daily reality)	**2 Quadrant of quality**
Low importance	**3 Quadrant of illusion**	**4 Quadrant of waste (Escape)**

Step 3: Produce your best work

1 Reflect on your study pattern so far:

- When do you work best? You need to do the most difficult work when your concentration is strongest.
- What time patterns suit you? Do you work best in short bursts of 20 minutes, or do you like to have at least an hour to 'get stuck in'?
- What is your best environment to work in? Do you like a quiet space or prefer to have music? Light, space and comfort are also factors to consider.
- How can you create the pattern and environment you need? What do you need to do and by when?

2 Which of the portfolio tasks seem to be easy and which are you most concerned about?

- Plan your work so that you make sure you don't leave those awkward and difficult tasks to last. Set aside good-quality time to focus on them.
- Equally, plan to give enough time to those that look easy so that you maintain your highest quality.

Step 4: Understand where your support is coming from

Who is involved in supporting you to complete your portfolio? Are you clear about their role?

1 **Practice educator**
   This is the person who will be working with you throughout the placement, and their role is examined in detail in Chapter 4. Generally they will be responsible for the teaching, supervision and assessment during your placement. In particular they will be enabling you to integrate theory and practice, develop your social work skills, consider your values and address issues of anti-oppressive and anti-discriminatory practice. They will be working with the university and so will be able to help you to understand and complete your placement tasks. Their support as you compile your portfolio will be invaluable: **but** it is still **your** responsibility. Use supervision to ask questions about how and what to include. You can be proactive by thinking about the imminent portfolio tasks before a supervision session and having questions and plans ready for discussion.

2 **Placement/work-based supervisor**
   You will normally work with a placement or work-based supervisor if your practice educator is off-site. The supervisor is the person who is 'on-site' – that is, who works in the same workplace as you – and will provide day-to-day support. They will work with the off-site practice educator. Although they are not normally responsible for assessing the portfolio they will often be a good sounding board for checking out your ideas for how to complete the tasks. But remember – any final decision should be checked with your practice educator.

3 **University placement team**
   These are the people responsible for your placement experience overall. They will support both you as the student, the practice educator, and placement/work-based staff to ensure that the teaching, learning and assessment are of a good standard. They will often be the people who designed the portfolio tasks, and in the event of any questions that cannot be answered by the practice educator, or that you are confused about, they are the people to check with. You will probably have recall days where you will get the chance to ask any questions. Again – be proactive – work out what you need to know to get on with your portfolio and ask the question.

4 **Other students**
   Your fellow students can be a great source of support, and talking through your ideas for how you intend to complete tasks can be really useful. Try to 'buddy up' with someone who will be supportive when necessary, but also challenging, and who is not afraid to ask tough questions and give constructive feedback. You may find that this brings a great learning opportunity for you.
   Remember, however, that other students can also be a source of misinformation. It is not unknown for a whole student group to invent a new interpretation of a task through a Facebook discussion. Always ensure you check back with the people who will be assessing your work as the final decision-makers.

Step 5: Review progress

You may have reviews already set as part of the placement. If so, take them seriously and prepare for them. If not, schedule them yourself.

The review will be about your progress as a learner and how well you are doing towards completing a successful placement. Be sure you consider both aspects. You are responsible for assessing your own progress and for informing others about aspects that are working well and those that are not.

- Focus on the nine domains of the Professional Capabilities Framework (see Chapter 2 and the Appendix). How well do you think you are demonstrating your capability in these areas? What evidence do you have?
- What other assessment criteria should you be considering and how well are you meeting them?
- How well are you progressing with meeting your own personal learning outcomes for the placement?
- What is the feedback from others?
- Having considered all this information, what actions do you need to take?

Step 6: Submit the portfolio

It is never too early to think about this stage, and to get prepared for the day you finish placement and feel a sense of achievement as you hand in your portfolio. You want it to deliver a message about how successful you have been in meeting the requirements of the course. However, some of the most common complaints from practice educators and practice assessment panel readers are about the physical structure of the portfolio and how well written it is.

So here are some practical tips to consider:

1 **The container/cover**
   It may not be the most important place to start, but in making your portfolio your own, find a folder that works for you. It needs to be the 'right size'. Consider how much needs to go in it. A folder that is so full that bits fall out is not a professionally constructed portfolio. Equally, one that is too large and heavy is likely to irritate the reader. What is on the outside? Folders do not need to be expensive and gold trimmed; but equally, a scruffy dog-eared folder with a teddy bear on the front is not really appropriate. Plain and simple is a wise choice, with the required identification clear and firmly attached.

2 **What's inside?**
   Clear demarcations between the different items is really important. Dividers are really useful as is a good index at the front. A portfolio is a bit like a file on a complex family with a variety of needs. If the paperwork is not in order you can waste valuable time trying to find an important document, and get very frustrated as papers are not where they should be. An organized portfolio demonstrates that you are able to keep good social work records.

3 **Be selective**
   Your portfolio is only a sample of your achievements in placement. Select wisely – ensure that you show your breadth and depth of knowledge and skills, not just more examples of the same thing. When considering what to put in and what to leave out, ask yourself questions about what exactly you aim to demonstrate with that particular piece of work.

4 **What to include and exclude**

Most programmes are clear about what should be included in a portfolio. Be sure you have complied with the requirements and included materials and evidence that clearly meet each directive. It is equally important to take out anything that is not required or irrelevant. Extra materials that are not requested demonstrate a lack of ability to follow guidelines. The composition of a portfolio has been carefully determined, and it is important you prove you can understand and respect the directions.

5 **Confidentiality and anonymity**

It will be essential to ensure that any reference to service users is anonymized. It demonstrates the value of respect, and is not to be taken lightly. What are the other programme requirements about confidentiality? It can take time, so leave enough to complete it well.

6 **Edit and proofread**

Proofreading and checking a portfolio is as important as any piece of coursework, and likely to take longer. Leave enough time to do it properly. You could make an agreement with a fellow student or friend to check it through.

Key learning points

- You own and are responsible for your portfolio, so make sure you produce one you are proud of. It is a reflection of who you are.
- Understand and appreciate the two main purposes of the portfolio:
  - *Assessment*: to judge whether you have reached the standard required.
  - *A tool for learning*: to be used throughout the placement to develop your social work knowledge, skills and values.
- Develop a positive attitude to compiling and producing a portfolio that represents your achievements.
- Find out what your support networks are and use them. You are not expected to know everything, so make sure you ask the questions you need answering in good time.
- Research, plan and schedule your tasks to complete the portfolio with care.
- It's not just about the end – it is also about the process. Enjoy the learning.

2 Evidencing your capability using the Professional Capabilities Framework

Kate Howe

Introduction

The basis for assessing whether you have reached the standard required to be able to practise safely and effectively as a qualified social worker changed in August 2012. At the end of their degree, social work students now need to demonstrate that their knowledge and skills meet the Standards of Proficiency (SoP) produced by the Health and Care Professions Council (HCPC 2012). These can be accessed at http://www.hpc-uk.org/assets/documents/ 10003B08Standardsofproficiency-SocialworkersinEngland.pdf. The Professional Capabilities Framework (PCF), developed by the Social Work Reform Board (SWRB), sits alongside these standards, and is designed to support social workers throughout their career. The PCF is an overarching framework that describes the capabilities expected of a social worker at different stages of their professional career (see the Appendix).

In addition, the HCPC has separate Standards of Conduct, Performance and Ethics that will be relevant to you when you register as a qualified social worker (HCPC 2012). The complexity of these different frameworks can be confusing, and the aim of this chapter is to offer clarification and guidance, so that as a social work student undertaking practice learning and completing a portfolio of evidence you will have a clear understanding of the professional expectations.

The chapter begins by explaining the relationship between these standards and their relevance to social work students before providing an overview of the PCF and its nine domains. Evidencing the nine professional capabilities well is at the core of demonstrating that, as a student, you have reached the qualifying level. The chapter continues with a consideration of what counts as 'good evidence'.

Finally, the chapter looks at each of the domains in detail, explores the meaning of the statements, the difference between levels, and the types of evidence you may use to demonstrate your capability.

By the end of the chapter you will:

- Understand the structure of the PCF and the relationship to the SoP.
- Know what types of evidence will enable you to complete a successful portfolio.
- Understand the composition of each of the nine domains, and the evidence needed to demonstrate your capability at each of the levels.

The Standards of Proficiency and the Professional Capabilities Framework

The language and acronyms in this new world of social work can be confusing and disheartening for a social work student trying to understand what they need to achieve in a practice learning placement. So let's try to demystify them.

The Standards of Proficiency are approved and monitored by the regulating body of social work – the Health and Care Professions Council (see http://www.hpc-uk.org/assets/documents/10003B08Standardsofproficiency-SocialworkersinEngland.pdf). There are 15 standards, each of which has a number of subclauses. Successful completion of your course will mean you have evidenced that you have reached these standards and can be registered with the HCPC as a social worker.

The PCF consists of nine capability domains, which are then divided into a number of different levels. You will often see it represented as a fan (see the Appendix). There are three levels that you will be concerned with:

- *Readiness for direct practice:* It is likely that you will have already met these capabilities as you are about to undertake practice learning.
- *End of first placement:* Each of the nine domains have a number of detailed capability statements that you are required to meet by the end of the first placement. These will need to be evidenced in your portfolio.
- *End of qualifying programme:* The nine domains have an increased and more rigorous set of capability statements to be met, and evidenced in your portfolio (TCSW 2012).

There are many similarities between the PCF and SoP, but they do have different purposes. Although the SoP is the standard that must be met by all social workers, set by the regulating body (HCPC), the PCF will be the framework used by qualifying programmes and employing authorities, as it has the continuity of career development.

To avoid any concerns that the SoP are not being met, the HCPC and The College of Social Work (TCSW) have mapped the standards against the PCF expectations for the end of qualifying programme level. While there are some differences in the language used, both organizations are clear that the overall requirements are the same.

Standards of Conduct, Performance and Ethics

You will be bound by these standards when you register as a social worker at the end of your course, and so they do not formally apply to you as a student. There are 14 statements that outline your duties as a professional social worker, and ensuring you maintain these standards as a student is good practice. They may even be used by your programme as a framework for assessing your fitness to practice.

Overview of the Professional Capabilities Framework

The Professional Capabilities Framework was developed by the Social Work Reform Board and is now owned by The College of Social Work. It provides a framework that sets out the profession's expectations for what a social worker should be able to do at each stage of their career. For students, it gives a clear structure about the standards you will be expected to achieve during your final-year assessment.

There is now a clear difference between what you will be expected to evidence and achieve at the end of your first placement, and at the end of the programme. The College of Social Work (TCSW 2012b) states that:

- *By the end of the first placement* students should demonstrate effective use of knowledge, skills and commitment to core values in social work in a given setting in predominantly less complex situations, with supervision and support. They will have demonstrated capacity to work with people and situations where there may not be simple clear-cut solutions.
- *By the end of qualifying programmes* newly qualified social workers should have demonstrated the knowledge, skills and values to work with a range of user groups, the ability to undertake a range of tasks at a foundation level, and the capacity to work with more complex situations. They should be able to work more autonomously, while recognizing that the final decision will still rest with their supervisor; they will seek appropriate support and supervision. These capabilities will have been demonstrated through the last placement together with the final assessment of other work in the qualifying programme.

This difference in expectations becomes clearer as we look in detail at each of the nine domains. However, the significance of this differentiation is to recognize the length of time in practice learning needed to reach the qualifying standard. As a student you will still have major areas of development remaining at the end of the first 70-day placement. The capability statements will help you to understand the progress you are making.

The nine capabilities should be seen as interdependent, not separate. As they interact in professional practice, so there are overlaps between the capabilities within the domains, and many issues will be relevant to more than one domain. The understanding of what a social worker does will only be complete by taking into account all nine capabilities.

The College of Social Work has made it clear that practice should be assessed '**holistically**' (TCSW 2012). By this they mean that you need to demonstrate integration of all aspects of learning, and show that you have an understanding of how all the capabilities are relevant and crucial to being a professional social worker. The assessment of your practice will therefore be taken as a whole, and will not be about meeting each individual part separately.

It is a like the assessment of a meal: you make a judgement on the overall presentation and taste, but if one part is disappointing – for example, if an ingredient is missing or of poor quality – then the final product will be affected.

Nine domains of the PCF

1 *Professionalism*: Identify and behave as a professional social worker, committed to professional development.
Social workers are members of an internationally recognized profession, a title protected in UK law. Social workers demonstrate professional commitment by taking responsibility for their conduct, practice and learning, with support through supervision. As representatives of the social work profession they safeguard its reputation and are accountable to the professional regulator.

Activity 2.1: Professionalism

> At this stage of your social work education, what does 'being a professional social worker' mean to you?

2 *Values and ethics*: Apply social work ethical professional practice principles and values to guide professional practice.
Social workers have an obligation to conduct themselves ethically and to engage in ethical decision-making, including through partnership with people who use their services. Social workers are knowledgeable about the value base of their profession, its ethical standards, and relevant law.

Activity 2.2: Values and ethics

> What are the main ethical principles and values that will guide your practice in your next placement?

3 *Diversity*: Recognize diversity and apply anti-discriminatory and anti-oppressive principles in practice.
Social workers understand that diversity is a natural and normal feature of all human kind. Diversity is multi-dimensional and includes race, disability, class, economic status, age, sexual orientation, sex and gender, transgender, and religion or belief. Social workers appreciate that, as a consequence of difference, a person's life experience may include oppression, marginalization and alienation as well as privilege, power and acclaim, and are able to challenge, support and advocate appropriately.

Activity 2.3: Diversity

> Can you think of an example from any aspect of your life where you have demonstrated anti-oppressive practice?

4 *Rights, justice and economic well-being*: Advance human rights and promote social justice and economic well-being.
Social workers recognize the fundamental principles of human rights and equality, and that these are protected in national and international law, conventions and policies. They ensure these principles underpin their practice. Social workers understand the importance of using and contributing to case law and applying these rights in their own practice. They understand the effects of oppression, discrimination and poverty.

Activity 2.4: Rights, economics and well-being

> What in your view are the three most important human rights, and how might you demonstrate these in your practice?

5 *Knowledge*: Apply knowledge of social sciences, law, and social work practice theory. Social workers understand psychological, social, cultural, spiritual and physical influences on people – human development throughout the lifespan and the legal framework for practice. They apply this knowledge in their work with individuals, families and communities. They know and use theories and methods of social work practice.

Activity 2.5: Knowledge

Make a list of all the areas of knowledge you think you will be using in your placement that you want to include in your portfolio. Refer to Chapter 5 for further exploration of this domain.

6 *Critical reflection and analysis*: Apply critical reflection and analysis to inform and provide a rationale for professional decision-making.
Social workers are knowledgeable about, and apply the principles of, critical thinking and reasoned discernment. They identify, distinguish, evaluate and integrate multiple sources of knowledge and evidence. These include practice evidence, their own practice experience, service user and carer experience, together with research-based, organizational, policy and legal knowledge. They use critical thinking augmented by creativity and curiosity.

Activity 2.6: Critical reflection and analysis

Think of a situation where you have reflected on your actions. What sort of questions did you ask yourself?

7 *Intervention and skills*: Use judgement and authority to intervene with individuals, families and communities to promote independence, provide support and prevent harm, neglect and abuse.
Social workers engage with individuals, families, groups and communities, working alongside people to assess and intervene. They enable effective relationships and are effective communicators, using appropriate skills. Using their professional judgement, they employ a range of interventions: promoting independence, providing support and protection, taking preventative action, and ensuring safety while balancing rights and risks. They understand and take account of differentials in power, and are able to use authority appropriately. They also evaluate their own practice and the outcomes for those they work with.

Activity 2.7: Intervention and skills

What skills do you have that will help you to intervene with individuals, families and communities?

8   *Contexts and organizations*: Engage with, inform, and adapt to changing contexts that shape practice. Operate effectively within organizational frameworks and contribute to the development of services and organizations. Operate effectively within multi-agency and inter-professional settings.

Social workers are informed about and are proactively responsive to the challenges and opportunities that come with changing social contexts and constructs. They fulfil this responsibility in accordance with their professional values and ethics, both as individual professionals and as members of the organization in which they work. They collaborate, inform and are informed by their work with others, inter-professionally and with communities.

Activity 2.8: Context and organizations

Make a list of the different organizations and professionals that you might be working with in your next placement and that you could be including in your portfolio.

9   *Professional leadership*: Take responsibility for the professional learning and development of others through supervision, mentoring, assessing, research, teaching, leadership and management.

The social work profession evolves through the contribution of its members in activities such as practice research, supervision, assessment of practice, teaching and management. An individual's contribution will gain influence when undertaken as part of a learning, practice-focused organization. Learning may be facilitated with a wide range of people, including social work colleagues, service users and carers, volunteers, foster carers, and other professionals.

Activity 2.9: Professional leadership

As a student it is probably difficult to consider this, but your personal experience and knowledge developed in your studies could mean that you have specific areas that are greater than other members of the team. So think about what you might do to help others to learn from you and your growing body of knowledge and skills?

What is evidence?

Evidence in the context of social work portfolios can best be defined as the **body of information** that will be used to assess whether you have met the required standards during your period of practice learning. But this may still be hard to conceptualize. Evidence in social work can have a variety of meanings: it may be the hard facts of having a case allocated to you, or it may be a reflective log, considering your actions during a particular incident. Evidence gathering is therefore complex and needs to be considered on an ongoing basis before and during placement.

The first step is to be clear about **how** you evidence – i.e. what **information** will you include in a portfolio to **prove** you have the capabilities to pass the placement. Many programmes set out what types of evidence are required as sources for your information. It is important that you are really clear about what **your programme requirements** are.

Here is a list of some types of evidence, and a space for you to make notes. Using your programme guidance tick whether each item needs to, or can, be included in your portfolio. If so, how many instances are required? And what other detail is useful to remember?

Type of evidence	To be included?	How many?	Notes
Direct observation of practice			
Analysis of practice			
Supervision notes			
Recordings of practice			
Summaries of work			
Feedback from professionals			
Feedback from service users			
Reflective summaries			
Critical incident analysis			
Case notes			
Assessment reports			
Learning logs/journal			

The next consideration is the quality of evidence you will provide. This is always a tricky area as the assessment of social work practice is not scientifically measured by value-free methods. You will already know that social work is diverse, unpredictable and complex, so providing good-quality evidence is not an easy task. There are, however, some questions that might help you decide whether the evidence is 'good enough'.

1 **Is it relevant?**
    Do you have a clear understanding of the capability statement you are evidencing? It can be useful to talk to your practice educator to tease out the different perspectives.

    • What is the connection between the piece of evidence and the capability statement?
    • Have you made it clear?
    • Does the evidence cover all or part of the statement?

2 **Is it valid?**
    Does the piece of practice relate to your experience in practice learning? Is it clear how your practice is valid within the agency context of policies and practice?

3 **Is it sufficient?**
Have you ensured that the evidence is of sufficient depth to meet the capability statement? What could you add to demonstrate your understanding even better?

4 **Is it reliable?**
Does this piece of evidence fit with evidence from other sources in your portfolio to build up a holistic and congruent profile of your practice?

5 **Is it agreed?**
Have you ensured that your practice educator has seen the evidence and agreed with your interpretation and description?

An additional method of judging whether your evidence is good enough is to use the concept of triangulation (Williams and Rutter 2010). Triangulation is when you have a number of pieces of evidence from different sources that prove the same capability. For example, you may demonstrate that you 'applied anti-discriminatory and anti-oppressive principles in practice' (Domain 3) in a reflective analysis of an assessment, as well as in a direct observation write-up. This triangulation increases the strength of evidence. Many programmes use this concept and ask for more than one piece of evidence in the portfolio.

Stages to acquiring your evidence

To be able to produce your best portfolio evidence there are a series of stages throughout the placement that you will need to complete:

1 Before the placement starts, or right at the beginning, spend time studying the capability statements for each domain at the appropriate level (end of the first placement or qualifying level). Think about how you might meet the breadth of the domain and what evidence you think you will be able to provide. The capability statements are not meant to be met specifically in a simplistic 'tick box' way, but give the range of behaviours that might be expected in demonstrating the overall capability.

2 Share your thoughts with your practice educator and discuss what their expectations might be.

3 In any written work keep a note of which capabilities you are evidencing.

4 After supervision, keep a note.

5 Keep notes of evidence and specific pieces of evidence in a folder so that you have an ongoing awareness of the quality of your evidence.

6 Midway through placement review how well you think you are meeting the capabilities. What does your practice educator think? What do you need to focus on in the next half of placement?

7 Make time towards the end of placement to review all your evidence and assess its quality.

8 Be rigorous in deciding which pieces of evidence **best** demonstrate your capability and to include in your portfolio, following the guidelines of your programme.

Evidencing the PCF

It is important to remember that the assessment is holistic, and your practice educator will be looking at your practice as a whole.

On the following pages we have set out each of the domains with all of the capability statements that are included at both the end of first placement level and the qualifying social worker level. By looking at the difference in expectations it is possible to see the progression a student is required to make while in practice learning, and to demonstrate in their portfolios.

Source: http://www.tcsw.org.uk/pcfDisplay.aspx (accessed 20 April 2012 © The College of Social Work). The PCF domains are reproduced here with kind permission of The College of Social Work. Please note these are correct at time of going to press. The PCF is subject to regular updating.

Activity 2.10: PCF evidence – first thoughts

Spend some time reading and understanding each domain and the differences in expectations.

Write down how you think you might evidence your capability at the specific level for your present placement.

What might be some of the tasks and roles in the placement that will provide that evidence?

---

1 **Professionalism**

End of first placement	Qualifying social worker level: Capabilities
1 Recognize the role of the professional social worker in a range of contexts.	1 Be able to meet the requirements of the professional regulator.
2 Recognize the important role of supervision, and make an active contribution.	2 Be able to explain the role of the social worker in a range of contexts, and uphold the reputation of the profession.
3 Demonstrate professionalism in terms of presentation, demeanour, reliability, honesty and respectfulness.	3 Demonstrate an effective and active use of supervision for accountability, professional reflection and development.
4 With guidance, take responsibility for managing your time and workload effectively.	4 Demonstrate professionalism in terms of presentation, demeanour, reliability, honesty and respectfulness.
5 Be able to show awareness of personal and professional boundaries.	5 Take responsibility for managing your time and workload effectively, and begin to prioritize your activity, including supervision time.
6 With guidance, recognize your limitations and how to seek advice.	6 Recognize the impact of self in interaction with others, making appropriate use of personal experience.
7 Recognize and act on own learning needs in response to practice experience.	7 Be able to recognize and maintain personal and professional boundaries.
8 Show awareness of own safety, health, well-being and emotional resilience, and seek advice as necessary.	8 Recognize your professional limitations and how to seek advice.
9 Identify concerns about practice and procedures and how they can be questioned.	9 Demonstrate a commitment to your continuing learning and development.
	10 With support, take steps to manage and promote own safety, health, well-being and emotional resilience.
	11 Identify concerns about practice and procedures and, with support, begin to find appropriate means of challenge.

2 **Values and ethics: Apply social work ethical principles and values to guide professional practice.**

End of first placement	Qualifying social worker level: Capabilities
1 Understand and, with support, apply in practice the principles of social justice, inclusion and equality. 2 Understand how legislation and guidance can advance or constrain people's rights. 3 Work within the principles of human and civil rights and equalities legislation. 4 Recognize the impact of poverty and social exclusion and promote enhanced economic status through access to education, work, housing, health services and welfare benefits. 5 Recognize the value of independent advocacy.	1 Understand and apply the profession's ethical principles and legislation, taking account of these in reaching decisions. 2 Recognize and, with support, manage the impact of own values on professional practice. 3 Manage potentially conflicting or competing values, and, with guidance, recognize, reflect on, and work with ethical dilemmas. 4 Demonstrate respectful partnership work with service users and carers, eliciting and respecting their needs and views, and promoting their participation in decision-making, wherever possible. 5 Recognize and promote individuals' rights to autonomy and self-determination. 6 Promote and protect the privacy of individuals within and outside their families and networks, recognizing the requirements of professional accountability and information sharing.

3 **Diversity: Recognize diversity and apply anti-discriminatory and anti-oppressive principles in practice.**

End of first placement	Qualifying social worker level: Capabilities
1 Understand how an individual's identity is informed by factors such as culture, economic status, family composition, life experiences and characteristics, and take account of these to understand their experiences. 2 With reference to current legislative requirements, recognize personal and organizational discrimination and oppression, and identify ways in which they might be challenged. 3 Recognize and, with support, manage the impact on people of the power invested in your role.	1 Understand how an individual's identity is informed by factors such as culture, economic status, family composition, life experiences and characteristics, and take account of these to understand their experiences, questioning assumptions where necessary. 2 With reference to current legislative requirements, recognize personal and organizational discrimination and oppression and, with guidance, make use of a range of approaches to challenge them. 3 Recognize and manage the impact on people of the power invested in your role.

4 **Rights, justice and economic well-being: Advance human rights and promote social justice and economic well-being.**

End of first placement	Qualifying social worker level: Capabilities
1 Understand and, with support, apply in practice the principles of social justice, inclusion and equality. 2 Understand how legislation and guidance can advance or constrain people's rights. 3 Work within the principles of human and civil rights and equalities legislation. 4 Recognize the impact of poverty and social exclusion and promote enhanced economic status through access to education, work, housing, health services and welfare benefits. 5 Recognize the value of independent advocacy.	1 Understand, identify and apply in practice the principles of social justice, inclusion and equality. 2 Understand how legislation and guidance can advance or constrain people's rights, and recognize how the law may be used to protect or advance their rights and entitlements. 3 Work within the principles of human and civil rights and equalities legislation, differentiating and beginning to work with absolute, qualified and competing rights and differing needs and perspectives. 4 Recognize the impact of poverty and social exclusion and promote enhanced economic status through access to education, work, housing, health services and welfare benefit. 5 Recognize the value of – and aid access to – independent advocacy.

5 **Knowledge: Apply knowledge of social sciences, law and social work practice theory.**

End of first placement	Qualifying social worker level: Capabilities
1 With guidance, apply research, theory and knowledge from sociology, social policy, psychology, health, and human growth and development to social work practice. 2 Understand the legal and policy frameworks and guidance that inform and mandate social work practice, relevant to placement setting.	1 Demonstrate a critical understanding of the application to social work of research, theory and knowledge from sociology, social policy, psychology and health. 2 Demonstrate a critical understanding of the legal and policy frameworks and guidance that inform and mandate social work practice, recognizing the scope for professional judgement. 3 Demonstrate and apply to practice a working knowledge of human growth and development throughout the life course.

End of first placement	Qualifying social worker level: Capabilities
3 Understand forms of harm, their impact on people, and the implications for practice. 4 Apply knowledge from a range of theories and models for social work intervention with individuals, families, groups and communities, and the methods derived from them. 5 Value and take account of the expertise of service users and carers and professionals.	4 Recognize the short- and long-term impact of psychological, socio-economic, environmental and physiological factors on people's lives, taking into account age and development, and how this informs practice. 5 Recognize how systemic approaches can be used to understand the person-in-the-environment, and inform your practice. 6 Acknowledge the centrality of relationships for people and the key concepts of attachment, separation, loss, change and resilience. 7 Understand forms of harm, their impact on people, and the implications for practice, drawing on concepts of strength, resilience, vulnerability, risk and resistance, and apply to practice. 8 Demonstrate a critical knowledge of the range of theories and models for social work intervention with individuals, families, groups and communities, and the methods derived from them. 9 Demonstrate a critical understanding of social welfare policy, its evolution, implementation and impact on people, social work, other professions, and inter-agency working. 10 Recognize the contribution, and begin to make use of, research to inform practice. 11 Demonstrate a critical understanding of research methods. 12 Value and take account of the expertise of service users, carers and professionals.

6 **Critical reflection and analysis: Apply critical reflection and analysis to inform and provide a rationale for professional decision-making.**

End of first placement	Qualifying social worker level: Capabilities
1 Recognize the importance of applying imagination, creativity and curiosity to practice. 2 Inform decision-making by identifying and gathering information from more than one source and, with support, question its reliability and validity. 3 With guidance, use reflection and analysis in practice.	1 Apply imagination, creativity and curiosity to practice. 2 Inform decision-making by identifying and gathering information from multiple sources, actively seeking new sources. 3 With support, rigorously question and evaluate the reliability and validity of information from different sources.

End of first placement	Qualifying social worker level: Capabilities
4 With guidance, understand how to evaluate and review hypotheses in response to information available at the time, and apply in practice with support. 5 With guidance, use evidence to inform decisions.	4 Demonstrate a capacity for logical, systematic, critical and reflective reasoning, and apply the theories and techniques of reflective practice. 5 Know how to formulate, test, evaluate, and review hypotheses in response to information available at the time, and apply in practice. 6 Begin to formulate and make explicit evidence-informed judgements and justifiable decisions.

7 **Intervention and skills: Use judgement and authority to intervene with individuals, families and communities to promote independence, provide support and prevent harm, neglect and abuse.**

End of first placement	Qualifying social worker level: Capabilities
1 With guidance, use a range of verbal, non-verbal and written methods of communication relevant to the placement. 2 With guidance, communicate information, advice, instruction and opinion so as to advocate, influence and persuade. 3 Demonstrate the ability to build and conclude compassionate and effective relationships appropriate to the placement setting. 4 With guidance, demonstrate an holistic approach to the identification of needs, circumstances, rights, strengths and risks. 5 Identify and use appropriate frameworks to assess, give meaning to, plan, implement and review effective interventions, and evaluate the outcomes. 6 With guidance, use a planned and structured approach, informed by at least two social work methods and models.	1 Identify and apply a range of verbal, non-verbal and written methods of communication and adapt them in line with people's age, comprehension and culture. 2 Be able to communicate information, advice, instruction and professional opinion so as to advocate, influence and persuade. 3 Demonstrate the ability to engage with people, and build, manage, sustain and conclude compassionate and effective relationships. 4 Demonstrate an holistic approach to the identification of needs, circumstances, rights, strengths and risks. 5 Select and use appropriate frameworks to assess, give meaning to, plan, implement and review effective interventions, and evaluate the outcomes in partnership with service users. 6 Use a planned and structured approach, informed by social work methods, models and tools, to promote positive change and independence, and to prevent harm.

End of first placement	Qualifying social worker level: Capabilities
7 Recognize the importance of community resources, groups and networks for individuals. 8 Demonstrate skills in recording and report writing appropriate to the setting. 9 With guidance, demonstrate skills in sharing information appropriately and respectfully. 10 Demonstrate awareness of the impact of multiple factors, changing circumstances and uncertainty in people's lives. 11 With guidance, understand the authority of the social work role. 12 With guidance, identify the factors that may create or exacerbate risk to individuals, their families or carers, to the public or to professionals, including yourself. 13 With guidance, identify appropriate responses to safeguard vulnerable people.	7 Recognize how the development of community resources, groups and networks enhance outcomes for individuals. 8 Maintain accurate, comprehensible, succinct and timely records and reports in accordance with applicable legislation, protocols and guidelines, to support professional judgement and organizational responsibilities. 9 Demonstrate skills in sharing information appropriately and respectfully. 10 Recognize complexity, multiple factors, changing circumstances and uncertainty in people's lives, to be able to prioritize your intervention. 11 Understand the authority of the social work role and begin to use this appropriately as an accountable professional. 12 Recognize the factors that create or exacerbate risk to individuals, their families or carers, to the public or to professionals, including yourself, and contribute to the assessment and management of risk. 13 With support, identify appropriate responses to safeguard vulnerable people and promote their well-being.

8 **Contexts and organizations: Engage with, inform, and adapt to changing contexts that shape practice. Operate effectively within own organizational frameworks and contribute to the development of services and organizations. Operate effectively within multi-agency and inter-professional partnerships and settings.**

End of first placement	Qualifying social worker level: Capabilities
1 With guidance, recognize that social work operates within, and responds to, changing economic, social, political and organizational contexts. 2 With guidance, understand legal obligations, structures and behaviours within organizations and how these impact on policy, procedure and practice.	1 Recognize that social work operates within, and responds to, changing economic, social, political and organizational contexts 2 Understand the roles and responsibilities of social workers in a range of organizations, lines of accountability, and the boundaries of professional autonomy and discretion.

End of first placement	Qualifying social worker level: Capabilities
3 With guidance, work within the organizational context of your placement setting and understand the lines of accountability. 4 Understand and respect the role of others within the organization and work effectively with them. 5 Take responsibility for your role and impact within teams and, with guidance, contribute positively to teamworking. 6 Understand the inter-agency, multidisciplinary and inter-professional dimensions to practice and, with guidance, demonstrate partnership working.	3 Understand legal obligations, structures and behaviours within organizations, and how these impact on policy, procedure and practice. 4 Be able to work within an organization's remit and contribute to its evaluation and development. 5 Understand and respect the role of others within the organization and work effectively with them. 6 Take responsibility for your role and impact within teams and be able to contribute positively to effective teamworking. 7 Understand the inter-agency, multidisciplinary and inter-professional dimensions to practice, and demonstrate effective partnership working.

9 **Professional leadership: Take responsibility for the professional learning and development of others through supervision, mentoring, assessing, research, teaching, leadership and management.**

End of first placement	Qualifying social worker level: Capabilities
1 Identify how professional leadership in social work can enhance practice. 2 Recognize the value of sharing and supporting the learning and development of others.	1 Recognize the importance of, and begin to demonstrate, professional leadership as a social worker. 2 Recognize the value of, and contribute to supporting, the learning and development of others.

Key learning points

- There are two bases for assessing your capability to be a qualified social worker: the Standards of Proficiency set out by the Health Care Professions Council, and the Professional Capabilities Framework developed by The College of Social Work. They are similar in principle, and it is important to familiarize yourself with the key areas of knowledge, skills and values that you will be expected to demonstrate in your portfolio.
- It is important to collect good-quality evidence for your portfolio to demonstrate your capability.
- Developing an understanding about what will be good evidence in your placement, and planning how you will demonstrate your skills, knowledge and values takes time, preparation and organization.

3 Making sense of yourself as a learner

Lee-Ann Fenge

Introduction

This chapter aims to help you make sense of yourself as a learner by exploring how you learn. As a social work student you will need to develop a range of approaches to learning which adapt to the changing contexts of your degree programme, and span both taught and practice elements. As you progress through your degree programme your learning needs and learning style may also change. As you develop your portfolio you will be able to focus on yourself as a learner, the role of your own approach to learning, and how your learning style helps you to 'integrate your professional identity' through practice experiences (Alvarez and Moxley 2004: 88). A key part of this process is learning to integrate and reflect upon both academic learning and experiential learning from the workplace (Graham and Megarry 2005).

To start this process it is useful to reflect upon the skills and attributes you already have, and those which you hope to develop through your placement learning. You therefore need to consider what you bring to the placement in terms of your experience, skills, knowledge etc., what you hope to gain from the placement in terms of learning experiences and opportunities, and the types of learning experiences you prefer. You can develop a list to illustrate what you can offer and what you hope the placement can offer you.

By the end of this chapter you will:

- Understand yourself as a learner.
- Be able to identify which learning style suits you.
- Be able to use a learning log/diary to support your portfolio development.

Activity 3.1: Valuing your own experience

This activity enables you to value your own experience, as well as highlight the opportunities which may enable you to develop as a student practitioner. It encourages you to be proactive as a learner, and to take responsibility for your own learning and progress while on placement.

What you offer to the placement	What you hope the placement can offer you

Learning style

In simple terms, learning style can be understood as 'the typical ways a person behaves, feels, and processes information in learning situations' (Sims and Sims 1995: 194). This is the way in which you learn to process and retain information, and also the ways in which you use and apply knowledge in practice. As we have seen, it is your responsibility to select and produce material which demonstrates the depth and breadth of your learning during the placement learning experience. The early part of your placement is often a confusing time, as you grapple with what constitutes evidence of learning in practice and how you can use it. The problem is not normally finding evidence, as this surrounds you all the time during your placement, but deciding which evidence to use to best demonstrate your learning. Your portfolio will therefore document the evidence you have chosen to demonstrate your learning, your practice, and the assessment of these elements. Your personal approach to learning will influence the way in which you engage with practice learning opportunities, and the way in which you approach the key elements of the portfolio. These include:

- Social work values and codes of practice.
- Using social work knowledge and applying theory to practice.
- Anti-discriminatory practice and anti-racist practice.
- Service user/carer perspectives.
- Professional Capabilities Framework (PCF).

As discussed in Chapter 1, you will be guided through your practice-based learning and portfolio development by your practice educator. You may also have a work-based supervisor or a placement supervisor who will be involved in your practice-based learning and may be working with you and their portfolio – for example, in verifying evidence if the practice educator is off-site.

The Social Work Reform Board Guidance Statements for Practice Educators (2010c) state that practice educators should:

1 Take responsibility for creating a physical and learning environment conducive to the demonstration of assessed competence.
2 Devise an induction programme that takes into account a learner's needs and their previous experience.

To enable your practice educator to support you in an appropriate way, a learning agreement is normally drawn up to identify your learning requirements and the opportunities presented by the placement, to enable you to demonstrate learning in practice. It is important that you develop some awareness of your own particular learning requirements; this may include previous experience you have, and your own particular learning style. Your learning agreement may be a key part of your portfolio evidence.

A practice educator perspective

It is important to arrange an early meeting with the student before the beginning of placement, if possible. At this meeting there would be an opportunity for student and practice educator to exchange some historical information. This would include previous practice experience and history of practice education, as well as some personal information. It could also include details of when and how the practice educator would be available to respond to ongoing queries. So this begins to identify how the working relationship might develop. Issues such as who takes the notes of the meetings and who they belong to might relate to expectations and/or previous experience. Otherwise things might become out of control!

Individual learning styles can be explored, and possible similarities and differences identified, in order to ease the processes of education and assessment. The student needs to think about what they hope to learn on the placement, and how the practice educator can facilitate this learning. There is a formal requirement of weekly formal practice teaching/supervision meetings which may be undertaken by one person (on-site practice educator) or two (off-site practice educator and on-site placement supervisor). In either case, it is the responsibility of the practice educator to enable the student to make links between theory and practice, legislation and practice, and to think about anti-oppressive practice, etc. Does the student learn best through reading, doing or writing? Do they need to practice through role play, or do they learn best by 'being thrown in the deep end'? These issues are usefully explored at the beginning, and any differences in style, once identified, can be managed.

The practice educator is the first-line assessor for the student, and arrangements need to be made about the processes required to achieve this. These will, to a large extent, depend on the programme itself and how much evidence they require/allow to be included in the student portfolio. It is important to explore how much input the practice educator expects, or is required to have, in the selection of evidence. Again, this is something that will depend on the student learning style and their previous experience, as well as the programme requirements.

Reflecting on your own learning style

As you consider what you hope the placement can offer you, it is also helpful to consider how this is influenced by your own learning style. We all possess our own personal learning preferences and methods of learning, and it is a useful starting point to spend some time reflecting upon how you feel you learn best. This is particularly important at the start of your practice learning placement, and this can be shared with your practice educator to help identify appropriate learning opportunities.

As well as considering your own approach to learning, and the particular learning goals you may have, the learning agreement also provides the opportunity to consider any other needs you may have. For example, if you have a caring role that makes particular demands on your time, or if you have specific personal circumstances that make travel difficult. These can be discussed when the learning agreement is drawn up so that some consideration of these factors can take place.

Before you start placement, and before you meet with your practice educator and agency to consider the practice learning agreement, it may be useful to undertake the following activity in preparation.

Activity 3.2: Exploring learning style and goals

- What sort of learning activities do you prefer?
- What sort of learning activities do you avoid?
- Do you enjoy the challenge of new situations?
- To what extent are you able to learn independently?
- Do you prefer to observe others before embarking on a task yourself?
- How do you approach applying theory to practice?
- What specific learning goals do you have for this placement, and why?

It may be useful to write down your thoughts before the start of your practice learning placement, and share this with your practice educator.

Successful learning

Successful learning has been described as being underpinned by five key factors (Race 2007). These five factors are described as:

1 Wanting
2 Needing
3 Doing
4 Feedback
5 Digesting

(Race 2007: 11)

The five factors can also been viewed as key features of your practice learning while on placement. These include:

- Your motivation to learn (i.e. why you are on the degree and your motivation to be a social worker).
- What you need to achieve to complete your practice portfolio, therefore meeting the competences assessment requirements of the social work programme.
- Undertaking 'hands-on' practice with a range of cases and scenarios in order to develop your social work skills and knowledge.
- Obtaining feedback from your practice educators, university tutors, colleagues and service users about your practice.
- Reflecting upon what you have learned, and how this will influence your future practice.

Your approach to successful learning will be influenced by both past learning experiences and the present learning environment you find yourself in. Your own personal learning history is based on your past experiences of learning and is influenced by emotional, cognitive and social strengths and weaknesses (Holliway 2009). So, for example, if you had negative learning experiences while at school, this may influence how you see your own potential as a learner and the levels of confidence you have to engage in learning. If you are someone who has always enjoyed 'hands-on' learning, you may be keen to get to grips with real cases as soon as you get into your placement setting, and you may relish what Schon (1987) identifies as the 'swampy zones' of practice.

The learning environment offered through your practice placement will also influence and develop your learning style. Working within an organization, and being part of a wider team, enables you to become part of a 'community of practice' (Wenger 1998) in which the wider team can facilitate and support your learning journey. The context in which your practice placement occurs is therefore dynamic, and one in which other people – including practice educators, other practitioners, managers and service users – all contribute to the learning milieu. This has been described as the importance of others in 'animating' other people's learning (Boud and Miller 1996). Chapter 6 will explore, in some detail, the involvement of service users in your practice learning, and how you might evidence this within your portfolio.

By keeping a learning journal you will be able to reflect on key moments on your learning journey where others may have 'animated' or illuminated your learning. It may also be useful to reflect upon the culture of the practice setting and how this influences your approach to learning. For example, you may reflect that your placement team is one that embraces opportunities to learn together through open discussions in team meetings, presentation of case studies, and other practice-based discussions within team meetings. This may give you the opportunity to share what you are learning to the wider team. There may also be pivotal learning points from your own practice with service users which have proved to be key 'aha' points in your learning journey.

Activity 3.3: The culture of your practice placement

In order to consider how the culture of the practice learning opportunity influences your learning, consider the following:

- How are new ideas/policy and practice changes communicated within the team?
- How are staff and team development activities managed?
- Are there opportunities for shadowing team members?
- How does the wider team influence your learning while being part of this setting?
- How are service user/carer comments fed back into the team?

Your placement learning provides you with the opportunity to encounter new and challenging experiences, some of which may unsettle you and leave you feeling confused or uncertain about your knowledge and skills. It is important that you learn through these experiences, and do not try to appear competent in every situation. Remember you are a student social worker on placement to learn, and you have permission to feel uncertain when faced with new learning situations. This can be illustrated through the conscious competence learning model which describes four phases of competence (cited by Chapman 2012).

Stage 1: Unconscious incompetence

As you enter a new placement learning experience you may not initially know what new knowledge or skills may be required. You may not be aware of the need to develop until faced with new learning situations which challenge you. To start to learn and develop you firstly need to become aware of your areas of deficit or 'incompetence', before you develop new learning and skills. You can begin to reflect on these areas with your practice educator.

Stage 2: Conscious incompetence

By reflecting on what you need to learn, and the skills you need to develop in terms of your placement learning, you will become aware of the 'gaps' in your knowledge and skills. This can be an uncomfortable experience as you may feel 'exposed' in terms of your competency in practice; but this is a normal part of the learning process. Remember that you are on placement to learn, so continue to reflect on your own learning needs and find ways of meeting these through discussion with your practice educator. Once you are aware of areas that need to be developed you can make a commitment to learn and practice the new skill, and to move to the 'conscious competence' stage. Within your portfolio you can reflect on mapping your learning journey through to the conscious competence stage through summative assessments.

Stage 3: Conscious competence

Once you move into the conscious competence stage you may be aware that you are concentrating and thinking in order to perform a particular task. So, for example, when undertaking an assessment you might be aware of the preparation you put into this, including the timing, location and organization of the assessment. You may use formalized assessment tools or formats to structure the assessment, but will also be aware of the importance of good communication skills, listening and attending to the person you are working with, and making sure that you adhere to the principles of anti-oppressive practice. The skills of assessment at this stage are not 'automatic', and you will refine your assessment skills through practising them, observing others, and feedback you receive from observed practice situations and your practice educator. This is the stage when you should be evidencing the Professional Capabilities Framework and completing your portfolio.

Stage 4: Unconscious competence

Once you have achieved a level of unconscious competence, it is as if your practice has become 'second nature'. Although this signifies a level of experience and confidence in what you are doing, it is also potentially dangerous as you may become complacent about your skills and practice, and respond without thinking about what you are doing. For example, while typing up notes on a computer you may no longer have to think about 'typing', and may be able to multitask while doing it. However, if your responses are unconsciously competent in practice situations, you could slip into bad habits or make ill-informed decisions. It is therefore important to continue to reflect upon your practice, otherwise you could slip back to a state of unconscious incompetence, as illustrated by Stage 1.

Activity 3.4: Conscious competence

Think through the four stages outlined above and relate them to your own practice and placement learning experience.

Chair of Learner Identity

While undertaking research into the experience of mature learners accessing higher education, I spent time reflecting on their learner identities, and as part of this developed a model called the Chair of Learner Identity (Fenge 2008). This model was developed from the Chair of Identity (Lake undated, cited in Waskett 1995), which was originally developed to consider the experiences of bereaved children and the impact of earlier attachment patterns on their experiences. I felt that the pictorial representation of a chair provided a strong image, and one that is particularly useful to pictorial thinkers. I also believed that there was some synergy between this original model and the identities of the mature learners in my study whose earlier life experiences influenced their learner identities and ability to see themselves as 'university students'. I therefore took the pictorial depiction of a chair of identity, and developed this further to consider a range of psycho-social influences on individual learner identity. In simplistic terms, this links into the impact of early socialization, the support that individuals receive from family, schools and wider social and policy structures, and the way in which these influence their self-concept and identity as learners. At the same time, experiences in the 'here and now' can compound or refocus learner identities, depending on access to new learning opportunities and situations, and the types of support available.

The students in my research study depicted themselves as 'second chance learners' (Fenge 2011: 380) who made sense of their learning journeys by reflecting upon the challenges and failures of earlier educational experiences. These experiences included both the culture of learning within their families and schools, as well as the structural 'educational disadvantage they experienced during the early years of compulsory education' (Fenge 2011: 381).

The Chair of Learner Identity (Fenge 2008) therefore presents a psycho-social consideration of a range of factors which influence our learner identities, and the ways in which we approach learning situations (see Figure 3.1). It provides a simplistic pictorial representation of the basis of learner identity, with the structure of the chair representing the types of influences on how you depict yourself as a learner. This includes both past and present influences. Therefore, when considering the culture of learning, this includes the culture of learning that has influenced you previously, and also the culture of learning available through the university degree and the practice placement, including those elements that may support or hinder your learning within these settings.

The Chair of Learner Identity can be related to learning experiences in the following ways:

1 **Structural influences**
   This includes issues related to your personal identity (gender, ethnicity, sexuality, values and beliefs), and also the systems in which you study and practice social work. It includes the culture of the university in which you study, whether you are studying on an undergraduate social work programme (BA/BSc) or postgraduate qualifying programme (MA/MSc), and the culture of the practice learning placement. For example, it

The Chair of Learner Identity (Fenge 2008)

1 Structural influences: gender, ethnicity, sexuality, values and beliefs, and the systems in which you study and practice social work.
2 Previous learning experiences.
3 Family background.
4 Personal motivation.
5 This represents the seat of the chair, and illustrates how multiple aspects of our identity are supported or undermined by the various 'legs' of the chair.
6 This illustrates the back of the chair, and represents the support systems available to the learner.

Figure 3.1 The Chair of Learner Identity

has been suggested that sometimes those who join social work degree programmes with a good deal of practice experience may be sceptical as to whether they will learn anything useful by completing a practice placement (Fox 2004). This may make 'the transition from experienced practitioner to student on placement somewhat difficult' (Crisp and Maidment 2009: 166). This will impact upon the way the student sees themselves as a learner within the practice setting. Therefore, at the same time as being a social work student, individuals may also be maintaining and negotiating multiple aspects of themselves in terms of the roles they have had, and the ways in which they view themselves as practitioners and learners.

2 **Previous learning experiences**

This includes experiences which may be positive or negative, and may be linked to confidence to study at a particular level or in a particular way. So, for example, if you have had limited practice experience before commencing the degree, but have achieved well academically, you may have some trepidation about going out into placement and being assessed in the context of real-life practice. However, you may feel more confident about completing academic assignments within the university. Alternatively, you may have much practice experience, and feel confident in yourself as a 'practitioner', but may have previously struggled with writing assignments. In this case, you may feel more at ease about 'hands-on' practice, but anxious about evidencing this in a written academic format. This also relates to the style of learning you feel most comfortable with, and it is likely that a range of learning and assessment methods during your course may take you out of your comfort zone, building your confidence in new ways, and developing transferable skills. So, for example, being required to undertake a presentation to your peers may be something you relish, or something that fills you with dread.

3 **Family background**
This relates to the notion of 'habitus' (Bourdieu 1984) and the expectations you have developed of yourself as a learner. The 'habitus' is an internalized representation of early socialization and a product of our place within wider social structures. The ways in which we are socialized become embedded within our lived experience and choices. So, for example, if you are the first generation of your family to go to university, was this encouraged and seen as a possibility by other family members? Were you positively encouraged or discouraged in this aim? How did this influence your choice of course or university? Alternatively, if university is the 'norm' within your family, how did this influence the course you decided to study, or the type of university you considered? The impact of 'habitus' (Bourdieu 1984), and the predispositions this gives, may provide solid foundations or may have a more undermining impact on your learner identity.

4 **Personal motivation**
Your choice of social work as a career may stem from a particular experience or motivation. For example, if you had experience of the care system as a child, this may have nourished your desire to pursue a career in childcare social work. This may be a strong driving force in your choice of career and specialism, but equally it is important to realize that the degree is a generic qualification, and you are likely to be offered a range of diverse learning opportunities. How does your personal motivation influence your desire to achieve your aims, and in what ways does this influence your approach to learning? Your motivation to engage with the learning opportunities offered through your learning placement is ultimately linked to your aim of gaining a social work qualification. In my research, students expressed strong personal motivation to learn and study 'linked to the need to prove to themselves that they could do it' (Fenge 2011: 382). This is related to the need to challenge previous perceptions of ability, and can lead to a refashioning of learner identity so that the learner sees themselves as an achiever rather than a failure.

5 **The seat of the chair**
This represents the seat of the chair, and illustrates how multiple aspects of our identity are supported or undermined by the various 'legs' of the chair. This can be linked to your past and present learning experiences, as well as your future potential. It develops as a consequence of the discursive processes which occur within the socio-cultural learning setting (Gee 2001).

6 **The back of the chair**
This illustrates the back of the chair, and represents the support systems available to the learner in terms of the mechanisms offered by university lecturers, tutors, practice educators, placement supervisors, peers, and wider team members. It also includes the culture of learning within the placement, the support from fellow students and peers, taught elements on the programme, and tutorial or other support available. It embodies the knowledge, values and skills of social work, and how these underpin the practice you undertake. The PCF provides a framework against which your practice and practice portfolio will be assessed, and this also supports and guides the expectations of what you need to demonstrate through your learning.

The pictorial depiction of a 'chair' enables us to consider the foundations of our learner identities. If the legs of the chair are solid, firm, and of roughly equal length, we may possess a firm footing for our future learning and the identity we have of ourselves as a learner. We may feel confident in new learning situations and be able to see both the strengths we have as a learner, as well as the needs we might possess. However, if the legs of the chair are wobbly, of unequal length, or missing completely, then our learner identities may be shaky. In this situation it may be difficult for us to embrace the learning opportunities offered, until we address the cause of our difficulties. So, for example, if you encounter difficulties or are unable to cope with a situation, it is useful to explore the reasons for this with your practice educator using the Chair of Learner Identity. This will be explored again in Chapter 7.

A key element of the Chair of Learner Identity is how students make sense of themselves as learners in terms of their past, present and future experiences (i.e. in terms of how their practice and learning will develop in the future). It is therefore important to reflect upon the culture of learning and support that the student receives, to achieve these outcomes.

Activity 3.5: Chair of Learner Identity

Take some time to consider your own Chair of Learner Identity.

- What aspects of your own individual identity may influence the way you learn?
- In what ways have previous learning experiences influenced the way in which you see yourself as a learner today?
- How might your family background and attitudes towards education influence the way you approach learning?
- What is your personal motivation for social work as a career?
- What supports are in place to help you develop your learner identity?

Adult learning

Within the literature on learning, different approaches have been described. However, a key model is Kolb's experiential learning cycle (1999: 1 – see Figure 3.2) which is based on his theory of experiential learning. This is a developmental and cyclical process in which the learner moves from being an active participant in an experience, to being a reflector on the experience, then an analyser of it, before becoming an experimenter with new ideas. Although influential in terms of adult learning, the approach is not without its critics (for example, see Gardner 1996; Koob and Funk 2002).

In terms of reflecting upon your placement learning experience, you can explore positive and negative experiences in terms of how they move you towards new understanding. Often it is the situations which did not go as planned that can provide the most useful learning experience. This is summed up by Lam et al. (2007: 101), who suggest that: 'Although disturbing events pose challenges and trigger a sense of inner discomfort, disturbing experiences are also the necessary catalysts of reflective processes.'

So, for example, after completing a particular piece of work or observed practice you might reflect upon on your thoughts while preparing for the session, while undertaking the session, and after the experience. What have you learned as a result? It is equally important to reflect upon what did not go as well, and evidence this type of learning within your portfolio. Those reading and assessing portfolios often comment that students want to present portfolios with 'perfect' evidence. However, writing about a piece

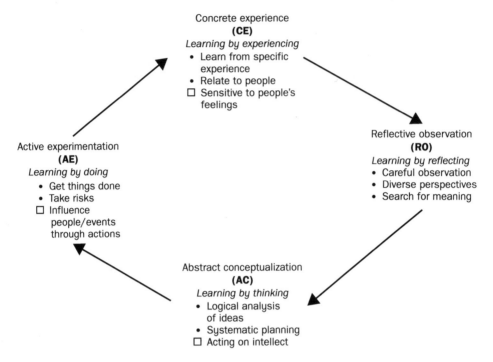

Figure 3.2 Kolb's Experiential Learning Cycle (1999: 1)

of work that did not go well, and reflecting on it, often evidences learning in a more powerful way.

A key approach to learning styles, which has been influenced by Kolb's approach, is identified by Honey and Mumford (1986). Four categories of learning styles are described in this model:

Activists: This relates to individuals who like to operate in the 'here and now'. If you are an activist, you enjoy new challenges and are quick to move into action. If this style of learning describes you, then you are likely to enjoy the challenge of your placement learning experience which gives you hands-on experience of social work practice.

Reflectors: If your preferred learning style is one that includes observing and evaluating situations from a range of different perspectives, you may particularly enjoy observing the practice of others within your practice placement, before being slowly introduced to these activities yourself.

Theorists: If you prefer to think through issues in a systematic way, assimilating different factors as you go, you may prefer a logically planned range of learning opportunities within your practice placement, allowing you to assimilate a range of information about the case you are working with.

Pragmatists: If you like to adopt a practical problem-solving approach to situations, quickly applying theory to practice situations, then you may enjoy learning opportunities where you can easily link theoretical understanding to the practice in hand.

Activity 3.6: Styles of learning

Think about the four learning styles described by Honey and Mumford (1986).

- Can you identify with any of these styles of learning?
- What might this mean for the expectations you have for your placement?
- How might these help or hinder you in your portfolio?

Expectations versus experience

The practice learning opportunities on your social work programme allow you to apply what you are learning at university, and are a potentially exciting element of the degree programme. However, a shift from university-based study into the workplace can also cause anxieties, particularly if this is in a setting completely new to you.

The portfolio also demands a different way of writing. Most writing in portfolios is reflective, and you have to shift to writing in the first person as 'I'. This can be challenging after writing more formal academic assignments. However, when writing in your portfolio you need to embrace the 'I' word.

Entering an unfamiliar agency may take you outside of your 'comfort zone', and has the potential to 'shock' you (Mackenzie Davey and Arnold 2000), which in turn may influence your own identity as a learner and as a student social worker. For example, we can often feel 'de-skilled' by changes of workplace setting, even though we may possess a wealth of relevant experience and skills which can be applied to a new setting. This experience may include 'a clash of expectation and experience' (Walmsley et al. 2006: 360) as you make a transition into the practice learning setting, but such circumstances can also provide very fertile ground for learning and personal development.

By keeping a learning log, you will be able to capture your thoughts and experiences as you enter your placement setting. Was it what you expected? Do you feel able to 'transfer' knowledge you have to a new setting? Have there been any key learning points to date? You will be able to use these reflections in your supervision sessions with your practice educator.

A student perspective

Keeping a practice log is a valuable tool for critical reflection. It helps to identify your assumptions, values and belief system which can help to determine what type of practitioner you are, and highlight the things that are embedded in your practice. It has helped me map my learning and development through my last two placements. It has enabled me to reflect on my cases, my practice, and helped me make sense of my thoughts, feelings, and experiences, as well as building and reflecting on social work theory. Keeping the log has helped me reflect on how I felt and the actions I took in certain situations. This enabled me to reflect on what I could have done differently and what I learned from it. It is really important to make the time during placement to keep this log as you can become absorbed in your role and not take the time to keep adding to such an important document.

I have drawn on my practice log when writing assignments and critical incidents as well as writing my work undertaken. It has helped me identify the achievements I have made, and write about how I was feeling during times when things did not go so well. Having my thoughts and feelings written down has helped me critically reflect and, because it is confidential, I am able to be completely honest and open about my placement and the experiences I have had. Not only does it help identify any gaps in my learning, but I feel that I would not have developed as a practitioner and have confidence in the decisions I make without keeping my practice log.

Key learning points

- As you develop your portfolio, you are able to focus on yourself as a learner, the role of your own approach to learning, and how your learning style helps you to integrate your professional identity through practice experiences.
- As you complete your portfolio, it is your responsibility to select and produce material which demonstrates the depth and breadth of your learning during the placement learning experience.
- By keeping a learning journal you will be able to reflect on key moments on your learning journey, and this can be a useful tool when pulling together evidence of your learning within your portfolio.

4 Working with your practice educator

Gill Calvin Thomas

Introduction

Previous chapters have started to look at the role of the practice educator in the student placement, and how you can expect to work with your practice educator when completing and submitting your practice portfolio. This chapter builds on this by exploring the purpose and processes in the relationship between the student and practice educator in more depth. The chapter will also look in more detail at the role of the placement supervisor.

We will start by identifying models of practice education and the roles and responsibilities of those involved. We will look at the role of supervision and explore it in some depth. As in previous chapters, there are activities throughout, and exercises which you should consider using with your practice educator or placement supervisor.

Giving and receiving feedback is part of the supervisory relationship, but feedback from other people within your placement can also be an essential element of learning (see Chapter 6). Constructive feedback will be explored, and a specific model offered to help you understand the rationale of feedback and how to make the best use of feedback for your learning.

This final section looks at how you can develop practice through use of constructive criticism, and in the face of negative feedback, in your portfolio.

Service user, student, practice educator, placement supervisor and tutor perspectives are offered to enrich your learning. In addition, links are made to the Professional Capabilities Framework (PCF) (TCSW 2012b).

By the end of this chapter you will:

- Understand the role and responsibilities of a practice educator and a placement supervisor.
- Recognize the different functions of supervision.
- Plan your own part in the supervisory process.
- Appreciate how constructive criticism can help you to develop your practice.

The practice educator

When you have been allocated your placement you will begin working with your practice educator. It is worth noting here that, from 2013, every practice educator will be a registered social worker and will hold an award in practice education (TCSW 2012b).

The practice educator framework (SWRB 2010c) sets out the responsibilities for practice education. The following domains relate to your practice learning:

- Domain A: Organize opportunities for the demonstration of assessed competence in practice.
- Domain B: Enable learning and professional development in practice.
- Domain C: Manage the assessment of learners in practice.

However, within this framework the practice educator has a multiplicity of responsibilities, as you will see below. Remember: you will be working with your practice educator throughout your placement period – he or she will be central to your learning, and therefore it is vital that you understand their role and use them to enable you to make the best of your learning opportunity.

There are two models of practice education:

1 The on-site practice educator works with you in your practice placement and will generally be a member of the team you are working with.
2 The off-site practice educator will not be working with you in your practice placement, but will be off-site and will arrange to see you in your workplace. The off-site practice educator may work with a number of students. When you have an off-site practice educator, you will also have a placement supervisor. Therefore you have two people supporting you – the off-site practice educator and the placement supervisor.

The practice educator – whether they are on-site or off-site – will have the responsibility to:

- Make themselves familiar with the programme, the practice handbook and assessment processes.
- Ensure an induction to the placement has been planned.
- Work with you and other members of the learning support team to negotiate the learning agreement, agreeing the processes within the placement, and your learning opportunities.
- Ensure that you have formal supervision for one and a half hours per week during the placement period.
- Work with you to help you develop skills in reflection, and written analysis, discuss your academic work with you, and help you to develop research mindedness.
- Carry out direct observations and assessment of your practice and provide verbal and written constructive feedback.
- Support you to create your portfolio and monitor the progress of your portfolio with you.
- Consult with you and other members of the practice learning support team on a regular basis to ensure processes within the placement are working for you and that you are meeting the requirements of the programme. Some of these meetings will be formalized, generally a review halfway through the placement period and a final review towards the end of the placement period.
- Inform the practice learning support team if difficulties are being experienced within the placement.
- Provide a practice educator report with a recommendation of pass or fail.

The placement supervisor

The placement supervisor has a pivotal role in your placement as they are the person responsible for the day-to-day management of your placement. Depending on the requirements of your programme and the level of placement you are undertaking, they may or may not be a qualified social worker.

The placement supervisor will have the responsibility to:

- Make themselves familiar with the programme, the practice handbook and assessment processes.
- Ensure an induction is planned for you.
- As part of the practice learning support team, take part in the learning agreement and all other reviews of practice.
- Supervise and support you in your placement.
- Observe your practice – this may be one of the formal observations and will also involve informal observations of practice.
- Participate in the assessment of your practice and offer you constructive feedback.
- Inform the practice learning support team if difficulties are being experienced within the placement.

The following section will focus on supervisory relationships as this is a key responsibility of the practice educator and the placement supervisor (if your practice educator is off-site). You may recognize (below) that supervision is an important element in practice learning and will aid you in presenting your learning in your portfolio.

Programmes have different portfolio processes; you must therefore ensure that you are familiar with your own programme and what is expected of you. You may be able to use some of the supervisory forms developed (below) in your portfolio, or they may simply add to your own toolbox as a way of presenting evidence of the Professional Capabilities Framework (PCF) to your practice educator.

Supervision

The Health and Care Professions Council (HCPC) stipulates that you must receive one and a half hours per week supervision while you are undertaking practice learning in your placement. In the first example of practice education above, it is your on-site practice educator who will offer you weekly supervision.

In the second example, the off-site practice educator will generally offer supervision in one week and the placement supervisor will offer supervision in the second week, which means you will always receive supervision from either your practice educator or placement supervisor weekly. However, you will receive different supervision in each of these models. This will become clearer as the functions of supervision are presently identified.

However, first of all, what does supervision mean?

What is supervision?

It may be that you have not worked in the social care sector before, and the concept of supervision is alien to you. Indeed, it may indicate something entirely different to you. For example, in the probation service a probation officer would supervise an offender, ensuring their compliance to the law.

Activity 4.1: Supervision

Reflect on the questions below:

- What does the word 'supervision' mean to you? Take a few minutes to jot down some thoughts and ideas.
- For example, does it mean a session in which your work will be scrutinized?
- Is it a session in which you will fear being told off for something you have done?

Kadushin (1976), writing about social work supervision, defines the three main functions of supervision as: educative, supportive and managerial. Morrison (2001), also writing about social work supervision, suggests the following functions: competence and accountability, personal support, continuing professional development, and engaging the individual with the organization.

Building on these models, we would suggest four functions for student supervision. As a student, your learning is the focus of all of your practice learning support team, but we must never forget that the service user is paramount.

Therefore, the first function of supervision is accountability. The second is to promote your learning and professional development. The third is to support you as a learner within the practice placement. The fourth function – and the one that links in with the portfolio – is the evaluation of your work, the assessment of your work, and the verification of the evidence you are providing towards the PCF.

Accountability and workload management

This function of supervision ensures that:

- The work you are doing is of a standard accepted by the agency, and that you are undertaking work according to agency policy and procedure. In other words, ensuring that the service user is being provided with the best possible service to meet their needs.
- Opportunities are provided which enable you to develop new knowledge and skills.
- The balance of work meets your learning needs. Too much work may be detrimental, not allowing you to spend time planning and reflecting on the work you are doing. Too little work may mean that you cannot meet the requirements of the programme, and as a learner you may become bored and stressed by inactivity. So the workload balance is important to enable you to provide evidence of your learning within the portfolio.

Professional capability and practice learning

This function of supervision ensures that:

- You have an understanding of how knowledge, theory and research underpins your practice.

- You become critically analytical of your practice and you develop skills to reflect before action (planning) and reflect on action.
- You are provided with opportunities to discuss values and ethics and to develop anti-oppressive practice.
- You have opportunities to discuss your continuing professional development.

Personal support

This function of supervision ensures that:

- You consider your work–life balance – how you are managing practice learning and written work for your portfolio, as well as all the other personal commitments you have.
- You have an opportunity to discuss your feelings about the nature of work you are undertaking and the impact the work may be having on you.
- You have an opportunity to reflect on maintaining motivation throughout the placement, attaining the best learning for you.

Evaluation, assessment and verification of evidence

This function of supervision ensures that:

- You are able to evaluate the effectiveness of your work.
- Assessment is a key element and is acknowledged. You should clearly identify the evidence linking to the PCF, so that assessment is rigorous and meaningful for you.
- Assessment is balanced over time, and you are able to map your journey to being consciously competent, and provide strong evidence for your portfolio as you become more knowledgeable and skilful in your placement.
- Evidence of the domains within the PCF can be verified as it is met, and added to the portfolio.

The model below (Table 4.1) shows how the different functions of supervision are used by an on-site practice educator, an off-site practice educator, and a placement supervisor.

Can you spot the difference between the on-site and off-site practice educator?

The off-site practice educator cannot offer you the accountability and workload management function that the on-site practice educator must fulfil. Therefore, it is vital that you also receive supervision from your placement supervisor, who will carry out that function.

Table 4.1 Different Functions of Supervisions

On-site practice educator	Off-site practice educator	On-site placement supervisor
1 Accountability/workload management.	1 Professional capability and practice learning.	1 Accountability/workload management.
2 Professional capability and practice learning.	2 Personal support.	2 Personal support.
3 Personal support.	3 Evaluation, assessment and verifying evidence.	3 Evaluation, assessment and verifying evidence.
4 Evaluation, assessment and verifying evidence.		

There may be some elements of professional capability and practice learning that your placement supervisor may also want to cover, depending on their interest, skill in practice learning, and time they have available. However, most placement supervisors see accountability and workload management as the most essential function because the off-site practice educator cannot be accountable for your practice in the placement and, as stated above, the service user is paramount.

Getting started

You have read about the responsibilities of your practice educator and placement supervisor. You have also read about the different functions of supervision. So this may be a good place for you to start thinking about what you want to get out of your supervision. Take a little time to carry out the following exercise (Table 4.2). When you go prepared for your first supervision session, you will already have begun to evidence your PCF.

Getting to know your supervisor

You could suggest carrying out the exercise below together. It is a good starting point – a way of beginning a relationship. Remember: you may be feeling de-skilled going into a new placement, but you will be bringing lots of experience with you, and it is important that

Table 4.2 Preparing for Supervision

Supervisee (your needs)	Supervisor
Where will the supervision take place?	Find a quiet room without interruption in the agency. Is this possible?
Do you want it to take place at a particular time every week?	How will the supervisor agree the agenda?
What will the duration of the supervision be? Remember, the HCPC say you have to have one and a half hours per week.	Do they have a prepared supervision agreement to discuss with you?
How will you prepare for supervision?	
How will the agenda be set?	
Bearing in mind the functions of supervision, what sort of items do you want on the agenda?	
What about confidentiality?	
How will you link supervision with your learning needs? Will you ask for feedback on your practice?	
How will you use supervision to help you with your portfolio?	
Who will take the notes?	
If a supervision session is cancelled, will you take responsibility to rebook it?	

Practice educator perspective
It is so important to start well with your student. You should value their strengths and give them the right messages – their learning is the most important thing for you.

your supervisor begins to map your strengths and understands how you learn. Your supervisor might have quite a different learning style to you, but they will endeavour to adapt and offer you learning opportunities that help you to learn best.

Activity 4.2: Learning something new

Answer the following questions, then move on to sharing the information and reflecting on what you have written.

How does it feel to learn or experience something new? Think about something you have learned to do relatively recently – how did you feel? The learning does not have to relate to the placement or work, but could be an exploration of what it feels like to learn a new skill – for example, playing a new game, or learning new IT skills.

- How do you feel when you do something successful?
- How does it feel when things go wrong?
- What do you think it will feel like to be assessed in practice?
- How do you react to stress – in yourself and in others?
- How will you look after yourself during the placement?
- Will you do anything differently now you have completed this exercise?

Being proactive in undertaking an activity such as the one above and mapping your resource systems will enable you to commence evidencing the PCF. It will also give you and your supervisor an initial idea of how you are going to learn best in the placement. In addition, by discussing how you both feel it may redress some of the power imbalance between you as the student and your practice educator/placement supervisor as an assessor.

A supervisor perspective

My student disclosed her feelings about being from a black and minority ethnic (BME) background. I admired her honesty, but I do think there is a danger of being knocked down if you become preoccupied with issues that might arise. But coming from a BME background might mean that there is a steeper learning curve. We have to understand that each student is unique, and the student is with us to learn.

We discussed some of these issues in supervision. Coming from a BME background myself I used myself as an example, helping her to see that some of her fears were inaccurate. Fear can be a barrier, but we have to remember that our experiences mould us as a person.

A student perspective

My practice educator was my rock throughout the placement. Among other things, she helped me with my work–life balance, telling me that I could not do everything!

I wanted to work with children, and really did not want a placement working with substance abusers because I have some family experience of alcohol abuse. I needed to recognize my own experience and the impact it has had on me. I had to bring it to the forefront and not pretend that I did not have that experience. I talked about all this with my practice educator in supervision, and began to see substance abuse from the other side. People don't want to hurt their families: it is the addiction, and they didn't make the choice to become addicted.

I also used supervision to talk about my day-to-day work. I had to go to a child protection conference and felt very anxious. My practice educator helped me realize that the agency would not have asked me if they did not have confidence in me, and that gave me more confidence.

I developed a real passion for the work, and did not want to leave. My practice educator was an important part of this.

Towards the end of your placement, when you look back to measure your own professional development, you will be able to see your starting point and reflect on how you have developed and managed yourself during the placement period. This learning can be included in a review, or in a reflective analysis, and integrated into your portfolio.

A student perspective

I was struggling with my written work. My practice educator ended up saying that we were spending too long redrafting written work, and that I was in danger of failing. My confidence took a real knock and I became quite frightened. What actually happened was that I started to gather knowledge about what was expected in supervision, and began to prepare for it. I began reading, and now recognize how much my practice educator has helped me learn. I have become less fearful about needing to know all the answers.

Using formats in supervision

Many agencies have a particular format for writing up supervision notes which might have an emphasis on accountability and workload management.

Depending on how you agree your supervision, you could promote the idea of using worksheets when reflecting on particular pieces of work. Indeed, you may be able to use worksheets as part of your portfolio evidence, depending on what your programme demands. Whether you are able to use worksheets within your portfolio or not, working with a reflective format can be a great way of critically reflecting on your practice with your supervisor. The supervisor can use the reflection as part of their assessment of your learning, and verify elements of the PCF for your portfolio.

Davys and Beddoe (2010: 88) suggest that supervision models based on learning and reflection help practitioners to 'adjust theory and practice to the ever-changing and messy shapes of the modern practice context'. As a student, it is so important for you to learn to critically reflect (see Chapter 6). Critically reflecting on the work you are doing is vital to ensure it is up to the standard required by the agency – in other words, is of a standard that meets service users' needs. Reflection will also form part of your supervisor's assessment of your competence.

Now, listen to what a service user has to say about students needing to be aware of their own feelings.

A service user perspective

We can all be naïve and susceptible to our own vulnerabilities. Students can feel vulnerable, even if they don't share it with their practice educator. It's partly the fear factor and breaking down barriers.

If a service user makes a student feel vulnerable and insecure, the focus of the impact can switch from the service user to the student. So it is important for the student to find a way to deal with their own issues.

They may not disclose how they are feeling to the service user, but the service user will see through their body language and tone of voice. The student could become emotional or defensive, and may not be aware of this.

Also, the student may not want to admit to being vulnerable. But I think they need to share how they are feeling in their supervision. Students should not try to go it alone because they don't know how it will impact on them as they progress in their career. It is part of self-development and self-awareness.

It is not easy to admit that things are affecting you. The student needs to say: 'This is affecting me. What is the best way to go about putting it right?'

The reflective supervision format below is adapted from Davys and Beddoe (2010) (Table 4.3). It may go some way towards helping you critically reflect on the impact of practice on you. In the model, the practitioner shows an awareness of the work described and is able to explore it by reflecting on the impact and implications of the work. It is at this stage that you may arrive at new learning and understanding. Moving on from this you begin to identify solutions in the experimentation stage where you will be reflecting on strategies and what you do next. This is followed by an evaluation and conclusion.

Davys and Beddoe (2010: 88) promote their model as a model towards learning rather than a 'blueprint for doing'. However, as a learner, it is important that you are able to plan and agree action with your supervisor. You can also link your reflection against the PCF, and have your competence verified on an ongoing basis. You will cause yourself stress by leaving the verification of evidence to the end of the placement. Ongoing work with your portfolio will enable you to develop professionally and help you feel more confident in your developing skills and knowledge (see Chapter 5).

At the top of the form you will have noticed the question: 'Who will write the notes – you or your supervisor?'. Supervising a student can lead to a depth of reflection which results in two-way learning: in other words, your supervisor will also be learning through the reflective process. However, for your portfolio it is *your* learning that counts! There

Table 4.3 Model of Learning through Supervision

Critical reflection and analysis	Agreed action	Link to PCF
Who will write the notes – you or your supervisor?		
Awareness		
How did you plan the piece of work? What was the task? What was the underpinning policy and legislation? What sort of method or approach did you use? How did you involve the service user? Now, think about telling the story and what happened.	Was your planning adequate? Do you need to research evidence-based practice in more depth?	Which elements of the PCF have been verified?
Exploration		
Impact		
What was the impact on you of tackling something new? Were your knowledge and skills sufficient to carry out the task? What impact did the service user experience have on you? What were you feeling when you listened to their story? You may have encountered something for the first time: How do you feel now? How did you feel about the particular approach you were using? What was your impact on the service user?	How will you develop deeper knowledge? How will you develop further skills? How are you looking after yourself? Do you need to do anything else?	Which elements of the PCF have been verified? Which elements of the PCF have been verified?
Implications		
Having explored the impact on you and on the service user you can begin to acknowledge what you have learned from the work.	Set out the agreed action clearly.	Which elements of the PCF have been verified?
Experimentation		
What do you need to do to continue working with the service user? What are your solutions? How have your arrived at them? Have you included the service user in your reflection? What are you going to do next?	Set out the agreed action clearly.	Which elements of the PCF have been verified?
Evaluation		
Have you arrived at new understanding? Do you feel freshly motivated to try out the agreed solutions?	Ensure notes have been completed and signed. Link with your portfolio.	
Conclusions		
Has the session met your learning needs? You and your supervisor can provide one another with feedback.		

is therefore some benefit in sharing the writing of notes in terms of evidencing *your* learning.

Writing of notes has to be balanced with you having enough time to explore issues. However, as you progress in your placement you will develop skills in actively listening, reflecting, and taking notes. This is an excellent skill for a social worker to have, and will link to the PCF.

Constructive feedback

Studying for your social work degree so far will have made you familiar with receiving written feedback. You will have received feedback from your tutors on your assignments, and may have received verbal feedback as well as written feedback from undertaking presentations. As a student, you may also have given feedback about your social work programme.

You are now going into an assessed period of practice where you receive feedback from your practice educator, placement supervisor (if you have one), members of the team, other professionals, and service users. So the feedback you receive on your practice will be about how you practice and how you might develop your practice further.

Hawkins and Shohet (2006: 133) define feedback as 'the process of telling another individual how they are experienced'. They also suggest that receiving feedback can be hard and can cause anxiety because negative feedback can prompt memories of being rebuked as a child, and positive feedback can fly in the face of ideas we might have been taught of 'not having a big head'. Reflecting on this suggestion with your practice educator may help you reflect on what feedback will mean for you, and begin the discussion of what will work best for you.

Davys and Beddoe (2010) tell us that feedback is best received when it has been asked for. Therefore, being proactive in negotiating that feedback will be part of your supervision, will give you some control, and enable you to increase your knowledge and skills. You can also negotiate feedback from outside the supervisory relationship – for example, asking team members and other professionals you are working with. Negotiating feedback from service users is also essential for your learning (see Chapter 6).

You will require support from your supervisor to identify the differences between how you might perceive yourself and how others might perceive you. Through this process you will begin to increase self-awareness (Walker et al. 2008). This is an important point, as feedback can sometimes feel painful and you may even feel that you have been misunderstood.

A student perspective

At the time I felt disempowered, vulnerable, and low in confidence, but I wanted to make it work. I took the criticism and used it to my advantage. I thought, 'These people have nothing to lose. They can just fail me.' There was such a power imbalance and thought I was not good at anything. That has changed now, and I recognize how far I have come.

Activity 4.3: Feedback

Now take some time to reflect on how you feel about receiving feedback.

- What sort of feedback have you received?
- How did it make you feel?
- How did you react?
- Could the feedback have been delivered in a different way?

Read through the feedback (below) given to F after a direct observation. You will see how the practice educator has focused on F's skills and values.

A practice educator perspective

F demonstrated kindness, which is an unfashionable and highly under-rated quality. Given the scenario it would have been understandable if she had made some sort of reference to her awareness of the service user's loss of insight into his abilities, especially as she was being observed. However, she chose to preserve his dignity and did not make any com-ment or inference which might have resulted in a sense of disempower-ment for him. The outcome was that the service user and his carer really opened up, and the interaction was undoubtedly an edifying and pleas-ant experience for them. F read the complexity of the relationship well, and demonstrated the kind of respect and gentleness which should be admired and valued within our profession. F's awareness of her own power, and the sensitivity she showed to a couple who were clearly find-ing their changing circumstances problematic, was kind, and I have no doubt she will make an excellent social worker.

Hawkins and Shohet (2006: 134) recommend a model for giving and receiving feedback, stating that feedback should be clear, owned, regular, balanced and specific. It is quite easy to remember, having the mnemonic CORBS. The model is reproduced below (Table 4.4), and adapted for a student and their supervisor. It would be useful for you, as part of your supervision agreement, to discuss the model and negotiate how you want to receive and give feedback which will help you learn best.

Receiving feedback

First of all, ask for feedback following the model above. When you do receive the feedback, listen to it all the way through with an open mind. If you find yourself becoming defensive, remember that you are in your practice placement to learn. Being defensive could also mean that you have misunderstood the feedback, so ask for clarification.

A supervisor perspective

One of the issues I gave feedback on was lack of critical reflection, which meant that the student was engaging in surface learning rather than deep learning. So when she carried out an assessment she did not identify all the relevant risk factors. She had been given opportunities to shadow other workers, but now we turned this round and I started to shadow her and also asked other members of the team to shadow her. We fed back to her what she had done well and not so well, and asked her questions. This really helped. She began to link theory with practice, gained knowledge and understanding, and became more person-centred.

Table 4.4 CORBS Model – Giving and receiving feedback

CORBS model: Giving and receiving feedback

Clear

Ask for feedback on elements of your practice rather than a vague generalization. Not knowing what you are doing well, or what you need to put right because of very vague feedback, makes you more anxious. For example, you could ask for feedback on whether you have used open or closed questions appropriately, whether your body language has been appropriate, and how you have utilized anti-oppressive practice.

Owned

Remember that the feedback being given is a perception of you based on what has been observed. It can say as much about the person who is observing you. So it will be helpful if the person who is feeding back uses words like 'I felt that you could . . .' rather than 'you did . . . ', which implies blame, and could make you defensive.

Regular

You will find that regular feedback will be useful to strengthen and sustain your learning. Negotiate feedback that you will find most useful. For example, if you are co-working with an experienced practitioner, ask that you give one another feedback as soon as you have finished the work. Another example could be following a direct observation of your practice. You need to ensure that there is enough time following the observation for both you and the observer to provide verbal feedback.

Balanced

Feedback that contains positive and negative elements is called constructive feedback. If you are only receiving very positive feedback, it may be that the person who is feeding back may find it uncomfortable to criticize. If you ask for constructive feedback and make it clear that you want to learn, this may empower the person giving feedback to reflect in more depth on what they are observing, and suggest to you how you might develop your practice. It is unlikely that your practice educator or placement supervisor will feel uncomfortable about giving you constructive feedback as they will have received training to enable them to offer balanced feedback. On the other hand, if you are only receiving negative feedback, your self-confidence will inevitably fall away. This may indicate that there are genuine issues with your practice.

Specific

It is not easy to learn from general feedback. You could ask your supervisor to give you feedback based on the professional competence framework. For example, your supervisor may have observed some difficulty in maintaining boundaries with service users; this could be linked to the professionalism capability – showing awareness of personal and professional boundaries. So specific feedback, based on what is required of you, will give you something specific to work on in order to evidence a development in your practice.

In supervision you may find yourself trying to explain why you did something. This might stop you actually listening to the feedback. So, begin by listening and absorbing the feedback before critically reflecting on it and reflecting on how you might develop your practice with the new insights you have been given.

Student perspective

I was persuaded because of a time limitation to go to see a service user without reading their notes. I made a mistake asking the service user a particular question when I should have known the answer. I had to work really hard then to try and get trust back. I learned from that mistake, and discussed it in supervision. No matter what the member of staff had said, I should have taken the time to read the notes. It was as though the attitude was, 'Addicts don't really matter'. Then I started looking around me and seeing how things could just slip. Leaving someone waiting for an hour: What did it matter, not offering decent coffee or a biscuit? What did it matter? Being able to reflect on this helped me learn, and I think I made a difference to service users in the placement.

Activity 4.4: Using feedback

How are you going to evidence how you have used feedback to develop your practice within your portfolio?

- How can you include your learning in the practice analyses you write?
- How can you include feedback in any reflective evaluations you write?
- Why do you think the integration of learning from feedback should be included in your portfolio? What does it say about you as a learner?

Unfortunately there are instances where issues have been raised and have not been resolved, despite the best efforts of all concerned. Your programme will have a process in place to deal with difficulties in placement that have not been overcome within the learning opportunity. You should read your programme handbook and ask for appropriate support.

You will be working with your practice educator and with your placement supervisor (if you have an off-site practice educator) throughout the time you are on placement. The relationship built within that partnership should, in an ideal world, lead to you feeling empowered and enabled to learn. You will have read in some of the narratives that sometimes the journey to learning can feel disempowering. However, the practice educator/placement supervisor will be there to support you all the way through. The result of your hard work will be the evidence that you are practising competently and meeting the requirements of your programme. The culmination of this whole process will be the creation of your portfolio evidencing your ability to be the finest student social worker that you can be.

Key learning points

- You are not a passive recipient of practice education.
- Gaining an understanding of your own role and the role of your practice educator/placement supervisor will empower you to look at ways that will help you learn best.
- Supervision will provide time and space for you to develop your critical reflective skills.
- Developing skills in giving and receiving constructive feedback will be an essential tool for your learning.

5 Evidencing the use of theory in your practice

Mel Hughes

Introduction

The practice portfolio is where you are expected to evidence the use of theory in your practice. This chapter explores the links between theory and practice, enabling you to recognize what theory is and how you are already using it, and wider knowledge to inform and evaluate your practice. It includes a range of tools and activities, along with tips and guidance from a practice educator and a student on how you can best demonstrate theory within your practice and, in turn, your portfolio.

By the end of this chapter you will be able to:

- Demonstrate an understanding of what is meant by relating theory to practice.
- Recognize the significance for your developing practice of being able to identify and apply a sound evidence base.
- Provide clear examples of what you base your knowledge on and how you can develop this in your practice and your written work.

Rationale for evidencing the use of theory in your practice: links to the Professional Capabilities Framework (PCF)

In 2008, the Department of Health and the Department for Children, Schools and Families established the Social Work Task Force (SWTF) to review the social work profession and to advise them on reform. The SWTF published its final report (*Building a Safe and Confident Future*) in December 2009. For qualifying social work education, it recommended increased emphasis on the need for more depth in relation to 'assessment frameworks, risk analysis, communication skills, managing conflict and hostility and working with other professionals' (2009: 18). The SWTF reinforced the need for three established aspects of social work education: knowledge, skills and values, but with increased emphasis on the need to enable students to make links between theory and practice. They argued that an in-depth knowledge base at the qualifying stage provided the foundation for high-quality social work practice and continuous development throughout a social worker's career.

The focus on evidence-based practice, and the need for social workers, including students, to draw on a range of knowledge and theory, was also identified by Munro (2011), who was commissioned by the Secretary of State for Education to conduct an independent review of child protection. Munro refers to the specialist skills and knowledge needed in children and families social work, and identifies how the substantial body of research evidence 'can help social workers make better assessments of children's needs and offer more effective help to families to create safer and more nurturing parents' (Munro 2011: 34).

Therefore, the need for wide and in-depth knowledge to inform your practice is to:

- provide a foundation for your ongoing learning and development
- help you to develop your practice
- enable you to identify issues and effectively assess situations
- enable you to identify and utilize effective interventions
- ensure better outcomes for those involved.

Professional Capabilities Framework (PCF)

In 2010, the Social Work Reform Board was established to implement the recommendations of the SWTF. The Reform Board had the objective of developing a system in which there are sufficient high-quality social workers to help children, young people and adults, in which social workers are well supported, and in which the public feels confident (SWRB 2010b).

> ### Activity 5.1: Reflecting on the need for high-quality social workers
>
> Take a moment to think...What does the SWTF mean by high-quality social workers?
> Make a list of how you would describe a high-quality social worker.

The nine key domains of the PCF have already been outlined in Chapter 2, and you can also refer to them in the fan diagram in the Appendix. The fifth domain identified is 'knowledge'. This chapter helps you to identify what knowledge, evidence, theory and research mean. You can then develop a number of strategies and tools for ensuring that you effectively demonstrate this within your practice and within your portfolio.

Conscious competence model

In Chapter 3, we introduced the conscious competence model. You were asked to consider your own development as a learner and to consider what your starting point was. It is useful to follow a similar model when considering your knowledge base and how you use this to underpin your practice.

Students at the first stage, **unconscious incompetence**, may not be aware of their lack of knowledge or skills, and may not recognize why developing a knowledge base, or showing how it informs practice, is important. Understanding the purpose and importance of developing a knowledge base is necessary to move on from this stage.

Students at the second stage, **conscious incompetence**, recognize the importance of developing a knowledge base. This stage, however, is characterized by 'not knowing'. The student becomes aware of what they do not know or cannot do, but is starting to make plans to develop the knowledge and skills to move on.

Students at the third stage, **conscious competence**, are able to deliberately put into practice their knowledge and skills and to be explicit about why and how they have achieved this. They may not feel particularly confident in their ability to do so, and it does not yet feel like second nature.

Students at the fourth stage, **unconscious competence**, feel confident in their knowledge and skills, and are able to practise these routinely. The knowledge is more in-depth, and the student is likely to be able to explain this easily to others. This is the stage that we aim for in professional practice, although it requires practise and should continually be under review to remain open to new and changing knowledge and situations.

Baum (2004, cited in Chapman 2012) added a fifth stage of **reflective competence** to ensure that that we continue to look at what we do and how and why we do it.

Activity 5.2: Developing conscious competence

Consider where you would place yourself in relation to practice learning and your placement environment. You can do this generally, regarding practice learning, or specifically, regarding a particular area of work you have completed or intend to complete on placement.

My experience in social work education is that students often have a wider knowledge base than they give themselves credit for. They will inevitably be applying this to their practice on some level, but may be doing this unconsciously. If this applies to you, you may need support to relate this knowledge base to your practice more explicitly and consciously. You can share with your practice educator where you feel your level of competence is, and what you need to move forward.

Explicitly making links between what you know and what you do (theory to practice) helps the person evaluating and assessing your practice and your portfolio see what you have learned and how you have used this to improve your practice. It also helps you to recognize what, how and when you are drawing on knowledge to inform your practice. Awareness of this will enable you to consciously make decisions regarding the effectiveness of what your practice is achieving, and also to question whether you are basing your judgements and decisions on assumptions rather than evidence and critically reflective practice. We will explore this later in this chapter. First, it is important to consider the terminology being used. What is meant, for example, by knowledge, theory, evidence, and relating theory to practice?

What we mean by knowledge, theory, evidence and relating theory to practice

Knowledge is 'what we know or are aware of'. There are many types of knowledge which can inform our understanding, insight and beliefs regarding a particular context or situation. As a social work practitioner, it is important to consider how we know something and on what we base this knowledge on.

Lee and Greene (2003: 5), for example, discuss learning in relation to multicultural social work education. They identify how 'students from different cultural backgrounds will have different assumptions about reality', and that when this reality is taken for granted and unquestioned, students will often assume that their world view is true and is shared by all others, regardless of their background. It is important to draw on different types of knowledge to consider whether what we know is true, and whether there are other ways of viewing a situation.

In academic and practice settings, some types of knowledge are valued more than others. Peer-reviewed literature and research may be considered more credible than other types of knowledge. It will still, however, reflect the perspectives of the researchers, the questions and focus they chose to take, and their interpretation of the findings. It is not enough to form the basis of a practice decision as it may not apply to the person you are working with. It is important, however, to be aware of the body of research evidence in order to ask the right questions, or to question or broaden your own knowledge.

Theory is a set of ideas to explain something. Loss and bereavement theory, for example, might help to explain a person's feelings and behaviour. It is only a set of ideas or suggestions though and, like research, may not apply to everyone. Theory provides a useful perspective from which to explore a situation or context, and can help improve our understanding and insight. As with research, the practitioner needs to use their skills to explore how, and if, it applies to the person or context.

Evidence shows whether the facts or information demonstrate a belief is valid or true. With regards to evidenced-based practice, it refers to practice which is based on credible facts, information and knowledge. It is used to ensure that the best possible assessment is made, and that outcomes are achieved by using interventions which have been demonstrated as effective in similar situations. The practitioner must use their skills to apply evidence effectively to each new situation, and should also draw on practice wisdom and other types of knowledge to reach this decision. Evidence can sometimes contradict other evidence, and so practitioners must do more than seek out the information to support their current view.

Relating theory to practice is relating what you know to what you do, and vice versa. It can include a wide range of theory, and is often taken to mean wider knowledge. Different terms are used as alternatives to relating theory to practice. Another term is evidence-based practice, as this encourages practitioners to identify the range of evidence used to underpin their practice.

Whatever term is used, it is important to draw on different types of knowledge and to use each one to question and reflect on another. For the purpose of this chapter, we will consider different types of knowledge and how you can use them effectively to inform your practice, help you make sense of a situation, and decide how to respond.

Activity 5.3: What do you know?

It is useful to remind yourself of what you already know. Make a list of as many theories and areas of knowledge you are aware of from your social work education so far. Your list could include theories, laws, policies, models of intervention, and others. Don't worry at this point about detail, authors or dates: you can check these out later.

It is likely you know more than you give yourself credit for. When providing an evidence base to your practice you need to show what your knowledge is, but also that you are drawing on this range of knowledge in practice. It is okay to 'Not know', as long as you identify this and are then proactive in finding the information you need.

Wilson et al. (2008) identify several types of knowledge that we inevitably draw on to inform the decisions we make in practice. They divide this into formal and informal knowledge.

Formal knowledge includes:

- research
- theory
- policy and procedures
- service user and carer perspectives
- legislation.

Informal knowledge includes:

- personal experience
- self-awareness
- 'not knowing'
- intuition
- practice wisdom.

(Wilson et al. 2008, 1999)

They recognize that, while different, all knowledge sources are of value and will interrelate and inform each other.

Activity 5.4: Drawing on informal and formal knowledge

Looking at the formal and informal knowledge wheels, how would you describe a social worker who only draws on formal knowledge?
And how would you describe a social worker who only draws on informal knowledge?

There is no one answer, but it is likely that you will have equated more personal qualities and values to the social worker relying on informal knowledge. The risks, however, are that this person's practice may be based on assumptions and judgements and may not lead to the best outcomes for those involved. Their practice may not evolve or adapt to national trends or research evidence, and may become out of date.

The social worker basing their practice on more formal knowledge may have been described as up to date, knowledgeable, and aware of effective practice. The risks, however, are that they may apply this to everyone and may not take into account the personal situation, feelings, or their own reflective practice or wisdom. This may lead to more rigid, formal practice that does not take into account the person's needs.

Effective practice will draw on a combination of different knowledge sources, and will use one to evaluate another. If considering a research study, for example, you can consider whether the findings confirm or challenge your personal experiences or practice wisdom. If considering your intuitive response to a situation, you can explore this further by comparing it to recent research findings. This forms part of the process of appraising information, but also in making sense of it. A high-quality social worker will draw on a range of sources of information to make sense of a situation, and will be open to different viewpoints and perspectives. They will be open to changing their mind and to broadening their knowledge.

Wilson et al. (2008: 100) suggest that 'the best professional practice will be informed by a wide range of knowledge sources that can be identified and accounted for and will be responsive to individual circumstances'.

Collingwood et al. (2008) make a distinction between knowledge to inform (to help you understand a situation or a person's world), and knowledge to intervene.

Activity 5.5: Theory to understand and theory to intervene

Looking back at your list in 5.3, which areas of knowledge would help you to understand a person and their situation (theory to understand), and which ones would help you decide what you need to do, or how you could respond (theory to intervene)?

Looking back at your list for 5.3, you may have included many different types of knowledge, including formal and informal knowledge (Wilson et al. 2008), theory to understand, and theory to intervene (Collingwood et al. 2008). At this stage in your education, some of these may be familiar to you. You may have explored them within an assignment, enjoyed a lecture on its use, or used it to inform your previous practice. Some of the models of intervention may be widely used within your placement setting – for example, motivational interviewing or solution-focused therapy. Others will be unfamiliar. You are not expected to have in-depth knowledge of all of these, and other theories, at this stage. There is an expectation, however, that your knowledge will develop as you draw on a wide range of sources to explore contexts, issues, and situations you encounter. Your practice educator can help you to explore these links.

Practice educator perspective

To help students understand what theory is, and why we need it in social work, I found the Collinwood et al. (2008) Theory Circle very helpful. All students I have introduced this reflective tool to have said it really helped them understand who the service user is, and what issues they come with (the kit), why we need theory/models/approaches in social work, and what the difference is between theories we need to know in order to understand where our service users are coming from (theory to inform social work practice) before we can actually plan for social work interaction (theory to intervene).

Students like the graphical representation of the service user and breaking down the different theories into understanding and planning for social work intervention. All students like using the graphical illustrations to make sense of what they need to know and how to go about working not only with the individual service user, but also some have used the Theory Circle with family systems and groups of service users.

Finally, another really useful tool is the internet and YouTube videos, which give excellent examples of what reflective practice is, and how to apply it in critical writing of essays. The only issue might be that most of these videos are from American university sources, so might be confusing for students. But if they can look beyond this they are good self-study lecture tools for students to access when suitable for them. The Theory Circle and the YouTube videos work well with students who have additional learning support needs.

Expectations regarding your development of knowledge and how you use this to inform your practice

It is useful to consider what the expectations are for the development of your knowledge and how you have used this to inform your practice. You can consult your programme information for particular guidance on what you need to demonstrate at each stage. This chapter focuses on the national requirements.

For all qualifying levels, the expectation by The College of Social Work (TCSW 2012a) is for: 'social workers to understand psychological, social, cultural, spiritual and physical influences on people; human development throughout the lifespan and the legal framework for practice. They apply this knowledge in their work with individuals, families and communities. They know and use theories and methods of social work practice.'

When you look back at the list you created for Activity 5.3, have you covered all of these key areas? Are there areas of 'not knowing' which you need to explore further? The College of Social Work specifically identify what knowledge is expected at different stages of qualifying social work education.

By the point of assessment of readiness for direct practice (prior to first placement), the words **initial** and **basic** understanding are used to describe the knowledge requirements. The aim is for you to have 'the basic social work values, knowledge and skills in order to be able to make effective use of first practice placement' (TCSW 2012a). Specifically you need to:

- Demonstrate an **initial understanding** of the application of research, theory and knowledge from sociology, social policy, psychology, health and human growth, and development to social work.
- Demonstrate an **initial understanding** of the legal and policy frameworks and guidance that inform and mandate social work practice.
- Demonstrate an **initial understanding** of the range of theories and models for social work intervention.

                                 (Knowledge: Readiness for Direct Practice, TCSW 2012c)

By the end of the first placement there is a stronger emphasis on linking this knowledge with your practice. The words **apply** and **take account of** are used to describe the knowledge requirements. The aim is for you to demonstrate 'effective use of knowledge, skills and commitment to core values in social work in a given setting' (TCSW 2012a). It is not enough to identify **what** you know; you need to show **how** you are using different types of knowledge to inform your practice. Specifically you need to:

- With guidance, **apply** research, theory and knowledge from sociology, social policy, psychology, health and human growth and development to social work practice.
- **Understand** the legal and policy frameworks and guidance that inform and mandate social work practice, relevant to placement setting.
- **Understand** forms of harm, their impact on people, and the implications for practice.
- **Apply** knowledge from a range of theories and models for social work intervention with individuals, families, groups and communities, and the methods derived from them.
- **Value and take account of** the expertise of service users, carers and professionals.
                                               (Knowledge: End of First Placement, TCSW 2012c)

By the end of qualifying programmes there is an emphasis on developing critical understanding. The aim is for you to demonstrate your 'ability to apply the knowledge, skills and values needed to work with a range of user groups, the ability to undertake a range of tasks at a foundation level, and the capacity to work with more complex situations' (TCSW 2012a). Specifically you need to:

- Demonstrate a **critical understanding** of the application to social work of research, theory and knowledge from sociology, social policy, psychology and health.
- Demonstrate a **critical understanding** of the legal and policy frameworks and guidance that inform and mandate social work practice, recognizing the scope for professional judgement.
- Demonstrate and **apply** to practice a working knowledge of human growth and development throughout the life course.
- **Recognize the short- and long-term impact** of psychological, socio-economic, environmental and physiological factors on people's lives, taking into account age and development, and **how this informs practice**.
- **Recognize** how systemic approaches can be used to understand the person-in-the-environment, and inform your practice.
- **Acknowledge** the centrality of relationships for people and the key concepts of attachment, separation, loss, change and resilience.
- **Understand** forms of harm and their impact on people, and the implications for practice, drawing on concepts of strength, resilience, vulnerability, risk and resistance, and apply to practice.
- Demonstrate a **critical knowledge** of the range of theories and models for social work intervention with individuals, families, groups and communities, and the methods derived from them.
- Demonstrate a **critical understanding** of social welfare policy, its evolution, implementation, and impact on people, social work, other professions, and inter-agency working.
- **Recognize** the contribution, and begin to make use of, research to inform practice.
- Demonstrate a **critical understanding** of research methods.
- **Value and take account** of the expertise of service users, carers and professionals.

(Knowledge: End of Last Placement, TCSW 2012c)

This gives an indication of what and how you should incorporate theory or knowledge into your practice, and how you can evidence this within your portfolio at different stages. The minimum requirement within your first placement is to demonstrate effective use of knowledge. This goes beyond listing or identifying **what** knowledge you have. You need to show **how** you are using this knowledge to make decisions about your practice. For example, how did you work within the law? How did your understanding of loss and bereavement theory help you to understand a person you were working with? How did this help you decide how to respond to their needs?

By the qualifying stage (the end of your final placement) the expectation is higher. As well as showing that you are using knowledge to inform your practice, you need to show that you can apply knowledge to a range of service user groups and within complex situations. This requires you to draw on a range of knowledge sources and decide what is relevant to a given setting. This requires a critical understanding. You need to question what you have based your assessment, judgement or decision on. For example, what do I need to know to understand this situation? What are the issues or concerns? What would be most effective in this situation? What is the evidence? What are the pros and cons of each intervention? What am I basing my understanding and insight on? Am I making assumptions? What is the value of this source of information?

A critical understanding recognizes the complexity of social work practice and that no one situation is the same. High-quality social workers can adapt their practice according to the needs of the situation, and often where there are conflicting demands and issues: for example, care versus control, or the rights and needs of the person over the rights and needs of the carer. This fits with the Social Work Reform Board's definition of capability. They use Price's (2004: 227, cited in SWRB 2010a) definition of a capability as: 'an integration of knowledge, skills, personal qualities and understanding used appropriately and effectively – not just in familiar and highly focused specialist contexts, but in response to new and changing circumstances'.

The expectation at qualifying stage is not only for you to demonstrate what you know, but to demonstrate that, with support, you know when and how to use your wider knowledge effectively.

Applying your knowledge to a particular situation or setting

Activity 5.6: Applying your knowledge

You are working with a parent with problematic substance use. There is an expectation that you will seek greater understanding, insight and perspectives from the person themselves, but also from literature and other sources. Take a few minutes to consider what types of information you could access to help you to understand their situation, any particular issues, and your response to it. What do you need to know?

Your list may include the following:

- Drug awareness/understanding of substances and their effects.
- Models of addiction/dependency/problematic use – e.g. medical, psycho-social models.
- Contributing factors to developing problematic substance use (Why might someone use? What might prevent them from changing their behaviour?)
- Treatment and intervention options.
- Research into the effectiveness of treatment options and interventions (What works best for who? And why?)
- Current legislation and policy regarding substance use.
- Current legislation and policy regarding parenting and child protection.
- Research and literature into the impact of substance use on parenting, and the impact on children. (What are the risks? What are the issues? What is the evidence? What are your responsibilities?)

Relating theory to practice is essentially about learning as much as you can about a given topic or area of practice from which to identify the best practice, intervention, and outcomes for those involved.

In your portfolio there is an expectation that you show some of this 'working out'. What were your first thoughts? Why did you think that? Was this based on an assumption, prior experience, or evidence? What information did you consider? How did it relate to the practice situation? What were the pros and cons of using this knowledge? How did different areas of knowledge help you to understand the situation; did it contradict or challenge what you thought you knew? Was the intervention effective? What have you learned from this?

Sometimes, when students are encouraged to 'relate theory to practice', students report being unclear as to what is being asked of them. Adopting a questioning approach by being curious, interested, wanting to know answers, wanting to gain insight, knowledge and understanding, and then reflecting on the effectiveness of the outcome, can lead you to the best evidence-based practice.

Claire, a final-year student, explains how this approach to learning has helped to develop her confidence, as well as her practice:

A student perspective

I love putting theory into practice because, as I write my assignments, I come across something that identifies with someone I know or an experience I have had in my placement. Quite often it just confirms what I already suspected, or helps me see things from a different perspective.

For example, I have learned how children who experience trauma are unable to process emotions. This has really helped me to understand so much about people I know and work with.

Understanding theory also helps me in practice learning and often gives me the confidence I need to make assessments, form an understanding in order to work anti-oppressively, and aids me in promoting change. If I did not have this knowledge and people skills alone, I would not be a confident practitioner.

I feel that knowledge is power and, used in the right way, will promote positive outcomes.

Mezirow's focus on instrumental learning and communicable learning

Mezirow suggests that openness to learning, from a range of perspectives to reinforce or challenge previously held views, involves learning which is based on curiosity and seeking to understand a situation. He argues that this is best achieved though engaging in discourse to achieve a best judgement (Mezirow 1997). He makes a distinction between content, process and premise reflection. The first two involve reflecting on your practice, such as problem-solving, evaluating a particular approach or intervention, and identifying the best evidence. He argues that this can lead to improvements in our practice and better outcomes for those involved.

Mezirow also encourages learners to engage in premise reflection, which involves reflecting and questioning the whole basis on which our views and beliefs are held, and what our knowledge is based on. This can lead to more fundamental changes regarding how we view the world, and how we in turn assess and respond to a particular situation. This can be achieved through communicable learning where, rather than focusing on how to do something (instrumental learning), learners also seek to understand the situation or context.

This is an important distinction when considering how knowledge informs your practice. To evidence your understanding and insight, you need to go beyond instrumental knowledge where you explain how and why you completed a social work task. You also need to reflect on how you questioned your own assumptions, beliefs and knowledge, and identify what you learned and how this enabled you to view a situation differently.

Activity 5.7: What is your knowledge based on?

Choose one of the following service user groups:

- Someone diagnosed with paranoid schizophrenia.
- Gypsy and traveller communities.
- People who are homeless.

Without further research or exploration, what do you base your knowledge of this person or group on? (tick all that apply)

- personal experience
- family upbringing
- religious beliefs
- work experience
- tv soap or drama
- documentary
- public perception
- radio programme
- newspaper articles
- an assignment you have written
- a lecture
- colleagues
- placement experience
- awareness of research findings
- a novel
- textbooks
- charity websites
- other things.

It is inevitable that, as a member of society, we will absorb information and knowledge from a wide range of sources. These may all provide us with useful information, knowledge, insight, awareness and understanding. Mezirow, however, warns of the risks of mindless assimilation where we base our knowledge on the 'assimilated beliefs, values, feelings and judgements of others' (Mezirow 2003: 1). A process of questioning these taken-for-granted beliefs is essential in ensuring that our knowledge base is open to the views of others, and integrative of experience (Mezirow 1996). You need to consider the value of the source your knowledge is based on, and whether this is your own assumption or based on credible sources of knowledge. Basing all of your knowledge about gypsy and traveller communities on a TV programme, for example, may give you insight into a particular experience, but is unlikely to lead to a balanced or entirely accurate view.

As social work practitioners we draw on our wider knowledge base all the time to make sense of a situation and decide how best to intervene. A high-quality social worker will ensure that this knowledge is based on a combination of formal and informal knowledge, and reflection on our own beliefs and knowledge, so effective practice can be achieved.

Evidencing your learning in your portfolio

So far in this chapter we have considered the wide range of knowledge we use to inform the assessments and decisions we make in practice. We have identified what knowledge is, and how best practice is achieved, by consciously questioning and drawing on a wide range of knowledge and perspectives. We have identified the importance of showing this 'working out' within your portfolio to demonstrate the evidence base for your practice and the process by which decisions are achieved. Showing these processes can help the person assessing your practice (including your portfolio), but can also help you develop your own reflective competence. The remainder of the chapter considers some strategies for effectively demonstrating this development within your portfolio.

How you incorporate your learning and wider knowledge into your portfolio will depend on the requirements of your particular programme. You may have to write assignments, critical incident analyses, and formal observation evaluations – or provide written evidence to demonstrate particular capabilities or standards. These are all areas where you can demonstrate the links between your practice and your wider knowledge (links between what you do and what you know).

When providing an evidence base to your practice it is useful to consider the links between different components. These are identified within the following model (Figure 5.1), which focuses on your development as an anti-racist practitioner.

Regardless of the focus, the model encourages you to make links between you, your placement environment, the service user group you are working with, the local community and your wider reading (formal knowledge).

Make links between

You
acknowledging your own background,
experiences and standpoint
consideration of your knowledge and
use of self;
your race, culture, values, beliefs,
experiences.

Wider reading
Specific research,
literature.
Public inquiries
relating to the service user group
you are working with.
Reading on anti-racist social work.

Placement
diversity within the agency
and the local population;
Agency policies,
culturally sensitive approaches,
your role.

Local community
Diversity
within the local population.
Specific cultural issues.
Local resources.

Service user group
e.g. race and mental health.
Cultural views on ageing or
parenting.
Perspectives of individuals you are
working with.

What does your learning from these mean for you
as a developing anti-racist practitioner?

Figure 5.1 Making Links

Activity 5.8: Making links

Identify an area of practice you would like to explore further. This could be anti-racist practice, as identified in the model, or another area of practice. Identify the key areas of knowledge under each heading (you, your placement, the service user group, the local community and your wider reading).

- How can you use one to inform another?
- How, for example, does knowledge of yourself and your personal experiences and upbringing inform your knowledge of the service user group?
- How has your wider reading added to, or changed, this view?

When writing about your practice you can demonstrate the depth of your understanding by exploring these different elements and the links between them. More depth can be achieved by not only supporting your statements with evidence but actually using evidence to explore, analyse, evaluate or reflect on your practice.

The following examples of reflective writing are based on three steps to achieving reflective, analytical evaluations of your practice which demonstrate your critical understanding.

Step 1: Description

I met with John to assess his needs. He has schizophrenia, lives on his own, and has never worked. I asked him what his needs were and how I could help. I focused on building a rapport and using good communication skills.

What do you think about the above statement?

The statement is accurate and explains what the student social worker has done. It sounds like good, competent practice in that the student social worker does not make an assumption about what John wants. They are aware of the need to demonstrate effective communication and inter-personal skills.

Step 1 does not, however, tell us why they have done it or what knowledge they have based this on. As we have discussed, consciously linking theory to practice helps you to recognize what has informed your practice and your decisions, but also demonstrates this to those assessing your practice.

Activity 5.9: Demonstrating wider knowledge

Read back through the step one statement. Assuming that this is your piece of work, how can it be improved in relation to demonstrating wider knowledge and the evidence base for your intervention?

Step 2: Linking each statement with wider knowledge or evidence

I met with John to assess his needs for the voluntary sector agency my placement is in. The agency bases all assessments on the recovery model (reference to your wider reading on this model and to agency policy). I was mindful therefore of the need to recognize his strengths and expertise; to share and discuss information to enable him to make an informed choice and to focus on hope for the future. The recovery model is based on the premise that two-thirds of people with a serious mental health problem make a significant or complete recovery (reference to where you have sourced this statistic).

John has a diagnosis of schizophrenia. According to... [provide details, with references, of what the diagnosis is and what the symptoms can be]: but the experience can be different for different people. I asked John how he views his diagnosis and in what way it impacts on him. This was to ensure that I recognized John as a unique individual and valued his expertise (provide a reference which links this with the values of the profession). I was also mindful of social and psychological factors which can affect someone's experience of schizophrenia (link to your wider reading on psychological, social, medical and cultural models of mental health).

The referral details identified that John lives alone. From wider research I was aware of a link between serious mental health problems and isolation and social exclusion (refer to research which identifies what these links have been shown to be).

The referral also identified that John has never worked. This too is shown in research to be a common factor for people with serious mental health problems (refer to research which has shown this). The research, however, has shown that this may not be because someone is unable to work, but because many employers are not willing to employ someone with a serious mental health problem (refer to research, identify the issues, and consider how this can inform your involvement with John). I asked John what his needs were and how I could help. This was to share control over the assessment process and intervention with John, but also to value his expertise. This is in line with agency policy (refer to agency policy), the philosophy of the recovery model (reference for the recovery model), and the person-centred practice/exchange model of assessment, which seeks to... (provide a brief summary of person-centred practice, or the exchange model, or the model you have based this on, with references).

I focused on building a rapport and using good communication skills such as... (provide examples with references) in order to put John at ease and develop a trusting relationship.

What are your thoughts now on this statement? If you were making an assessment on both pieces of work (Steps 1 and 2), which student would you identify as having wider knowledge and awareness of how this knowledge had informed their practice? It is only Step 2 where the wider knowledge and awareness is made explicit. Often, the main difference between students at Step 1 or Step 2 is just knowing how to incorporate theory, knowledge and evidence into their written work.

Making the evidence base explicit does require more time and effort. You may have to go away and find out some of the references incorporated into your written work, or work with someone else to help you identify what the evidence might be. Sometimes the wider knowledge gained from reading comes first, and can then be incorporated into your practice. At other times it is only when writing about your practice, or reflecting on it afterwards, that you become more aware of what the wider knowledge base is. It is important to be honest about this. For example: 'With hindsight I could have drawn on . . .', or 'Since meeting with John I have learned more about the links between schizophrenia and unemployment. This has enabled me to. . .'. This is all part of your continuing development and will lead to improvements in your practice and the outcomes for those you work with. As we discussed earlier in this chapter, not knowing is an important part of learning and competence as long as you are then proactive in seeking out the information or knowledge you need.

Step 3: Using knowledge to explore, analyse, evaluate and reflect on your practice

Once you have developed the skills in applying your knowledge to your practice (and writing about how you have achieved this), you can move onto Step 3. This involves using evidence to explore, analyse, evaluate and reflect on your practice, or vice versa, to use your practice experience and wisdom to explore, analyse, evaluate and reflect on your wider knowledge. You can do this by building on the links with evidence made in the second statement (Step 2). This can be achieved by adopting a more questioning and inquisitive approach. I would argue that the most important tool in a social worker's toolkit is the question 'Why?'.

In John's case, you could consider:

Why has he been referred?
Why does he live on his own?
Why has he been diagnosed with schizophrenia?
Why has he never worked?
Why is it important to see John as unique and to value his expertise?
Why is the agency's policy based on the recovery model?
Why is the government's policy focused on supporting people back to work?
Why do you want to recognize the social, psychological, cultural and medical impact on John?

Asking these questions (and others you have identified) helps inform your understanding of John and your role as a social worker supporting him. It is also part of your development as an anti-oppressive practitioner. Questioning **why** can enable you to:

- Develop a deeper understanding of John and his situation.
- Evaluate the information you are basing your knowledge and your decisions on.
- Identify the range of tools and interventions available to you.

- Evaluate legislation, policies, research and models of intervention based on your practice experiences – e.g. Does it work?
- Question your own values, beliefs and behaviour, and the impact of these on your own decisions and practice.

It is also important to consider how you answer the question 'Why?'. Earlier in this chapter we talked of the range of valuable sources which can be used to develop your own knowledge base.

Activity 5.10: Broadening your knowledge base

When considering why John has never worked, where could you look to find a fully rounded answer? Identify five sources of information.

Before deciding on possible reasons and factors as to why John has never worked, you could:

- Speak with John, as well as those involved in supporting him to discover their perspectives.
- Read his case notes and any previous assessments.
- Access literature and research on the links between employment and poor mental health, including schizophrenia.
- Access online resources, such as the main mental health charities, to gain first-hand views of their perspectives and personal testimonies.
- Consider the emphasis of legislation and policy in relation to mental health and employment.

Gathering this range of information to answer the question (Why has John never worked?) can enable you to develop a deeper understanding of John's situation, which in turn can enable you and John to identify and develop more meaningful interventions and support. The process of gathering information and asking questions can all be incorporated into written reflections and analysis within your portfolio.

Key learning points

- It is a social work requirement for you to relate theory to practice and to evidence this in your portfolio.
- Broadening your knowledge base will lead to more effective practice and better outcomes for all involved.
- It is important to recognize what you base your knowledge on, and whether this leads to particular judgements or assessments.
- There are different expectations at different stages of your social work education.
- It is not enough to identify what you know. You need to explore what your knowledge is based on, how it has informed your practice, and how you have broadened your knowledge to include a range of evidence and perspectives from which to develop best practice.

6 Visibility of self within your portfolio

Mel Hughes

Introduction

The practice portfolio is where you can demonstrate the depth of your personal and professional development and your awareness of the impact of self on your practice. This chapter seeks to demonstrate the importance of self within the process of learning and in social work practice, and includes tools and activities to enable you to consider your use of self and recognize your own personal and professional development. Examples are provided from students of how social work education has impacted on their sense of self and on their practice as a social worker. Suggestions and examples are included to support you in developing a personal, reflective and academic style in your written work, and practical tips are provided for developing appropriate evidence of personal and professional development within the portfolio.

By the end of this chapter, you should be able to consider:

- How you and your life experiences impact on the type of social worker you are.
- How your beliefs, values and experiences can both help and hinder effective practice.
- How you are developing, both personally and professionally.
- How your personal qualities, identity and social status affect your development as an anti-oppressive practitioner.
- How stress and stressful situations affect you, and what responses and strategies you have for managing this impact.

So try to demonstrate these themes within your portfolio.

Rationale for the focus on your use of self

Cournoyer (2000: 35, cited in Reupert 2007: 107) states that 'social work practice includes the conscious and deliberate use of oneself; you become the medium through which knowledge, attitudes and skills are conveyed'. As a result, social work education, as with other professional education, should not be restricted to the passive acquisition of knowledge, but must also focus on your personal and professional development. *How* you practice as a social worker is as important as *what* you practice. Use of self involves recognition that you incorporate who you are into your practice. Taking a whole person approach to learning (Hughes 2011a), your professional identity is informed by your personal identity, life experiences and values as you seek to understand new experiences and information by relating it to what you already know. O'Sullivan and Taylor (2004: 22) identify that, in life, we learn from a wide range of people and experiences. They define educators as:

Those who enable our learning – colleagues, friends, neighbours, parents, children, organizational leaders, spiritual leaders, artists, researchers, teachers, mentors – especially those who enable us to learn as we live and work and inspire us to a life of inquiry, openness and discernment.

In developing as a social work practitioner you need to be aware of who you are, what your knowledge, views and beliefs are, and how these inform your practice. The emphasis on *how* you practice as well as *what* you practice means that, in addition to being knowledgeable and skilful, you need to demonstrate personal qualities.

The emphasis on personal as well as professional qualities is acknowledged within various standards governing the profession. The Health and Care Professions Council Standards of Conduct, Performance and Ethics identify the need for you to behave with honesty and integrity and maintain high standards of personal conduct, which suggests that personal and professional qualities and conduct are not mutually exclusive. This is supported by service users and carers who have emphasized the need for social workers to possess personal qualities such as warmth, empathy, understanding, and who are punctual, reliable and trustworthy (Skills for Care 2002). Developing as a competent social worker not only involves developing your knowledge, but also how you use this knowledge. This needs to be visible within your portfolio. A perfect quote to illustrate the importance of personal qualities is attributed to Theodore Roosevelt: 'Nobody cares about how much you know, until they know how much you care.'

Activity 6.1: Reflecting on your personal qualities

Take a moment to think . . .

- How would service users or carers describe you?
- How is this different to how you would describe yourself?

An area where the use of self is important in social work practice is with regards to professional and personal values. Professional values, and the need to demonstrate an understanding of diversity, rights and justice, are central to the Professional Capabilities Framework. By the end of your final placement, you are expected to 'recognize and, with support, manage the impact of own values on professional practice' (TCSW 2012a, 2012b). This requires a degree of self-awareness and recognition of what your values are, and how your own values affect your judgements, in order to identify and reflect on this impact. This, in turn, requires a degree of self-disclosure which may feel unnerving, unfamiliar or daunting (Harrison and Ruch 2008) and so a safe environment is required for you to feel comfortable to be open and honest. This chapter includes a number of activities to help you to reflect on these elements and to develop your awareness of self.

Self-awareness

Self-awareness enables you to use aspects of your personality and experience positively within your social work practice, and to recognize where this may act as a barrier or hindrance. Lee and Greene (2003), for example, identify how students will often take for granted beliefs they have grown up with and assume that this view is held by everyone. They argue that social work education should enable learners to examine, question, expand and transform these taken-for granted-assumptions (Lee and Greene 2003).

The first step in this process is to consider who you are.

Activity 6.2: Step 1: Personal profile – What makes you 'you'?

Create a profile of what makes you 'you'. This should include aspects of your social status and identity such as age, gender, ethnicity, culture, religion, sexuality, health, class, educational achievements and roles. It should also include personal qualities such as your likes, dislikes, influences and interests, as well as your background.

You may want to consider aspects that you consider important, as well as aspects which may be important to others, or how others see you.

As part of the process of reflection, it is useful to consider what types of information you chose to include. Have you focused more on your positive attributes? Would others (friends, family, colleagues or service users) recognize you from this profile? Are there aspects you are more comfortable sharing than others? What are the reasons for this?

Reflecting on your profile and the questions identified will help you to consider your own identity: which aspects are important to you, and which areas you choose to keep private. Considering your identity and your profile from the perspective of others is a useful part of this reflective process as there are likely to be differences in how you perceive yourself compared to how you are viewed by others.

Luft and Ingham (1955, cited in Chapman 2010) developed the Johari Window as a tool for developing self-awareness. The model is made up of four areas:

- Open area: aspects of self known by you, and by others.
- Blind area: aspects of self unknown to you, but known to others.
- Hidden area: aspects of self known by you, but not by others.
- Unknown area: aspects of self unknown by you, or by others.

Self-awareness is thought to be developed particularly when seeking feedback from others to identify your blind area (Luft and Ingham 1955) or blind spot (Lee and Greene 2003,) and through critical reflection to identify aspects of your unknown area. Use of self within social work practice involves considering the information we choose to keep hidden, or are unaware of, about ourselves, and reflecting on its significance. Chapman (2010) suggests conditioned behaviour from childhood, and capabilities you do not realize you have, as information which is often kept hidden. He suggests that, while some personal information and feelings are private, those that are work-related should be moved to the open area to improve understanding and trust. The questions following Activity 6.2 can be used to help you identify which aspects of yourself are open or hidden, and to reflect on why this might be.

Consciously reflecting on your own identity, social status and life experiences can help you to develop self-awareness. This needs to be an ongoing process as you continue to identify aspects of yourself which may be open, blind, hidden or unknown, and to adjust these as you become more aware and more open. You may have experienced this already within your social work education, and be able to think of examples where you are more self-aware. This will be explored later in this chapter.

The next step, having considered who you are and what makes you, is to consider how this informs your views, beliefs and values.

Activity 6.3: Step 2: Beliefs and values

What are your initial thoughts, beliefs and reactions to the following statements?

- Blood is thicker than water (family should always come first).
- Children need more independence.
- Some people will never be able to work.
- All children should attend school.
- Older people are the head of the family.
- People with dementia are best supported in a nursing home.

All of the above statements are widely held views, but they are not universal norms. Not everyone will share these views, and there will be many reasons why you or others may agree in some situations but not in others. It is likely that, when considering the statements, your first thought was: 'It depends'. The process of becoming self-aware involves questioning what these beliefs are based on and whether others may hold different views. When you say, 'It depends', what does it depend on, and why do you think this?

Having considered your personal profile and how this is likely to have informed your views and beliefs, the third step is to reflect on the impact of yourself: the effect of your views, values, beliefs, and life experiences on different areas of your practice, in different settings, and with different people.

Activity 6.4: Step 3: Impact of self

In developing and demonstrating your self-awareness, it is useful to consider the impact of different beliefs, values and experiences on your assessments and decisions within practice.

Take the components identified within Activity 6.3 – family, work, school and care. In your personal life, what are your views and beliefs regarding each of these? What is important to you about family, work, school or care?

Purely from this perspective, how might this influence your assessment or your feelings of the following:

- A parent encouraging their child to miss school.
- A person in good health who has never worked.
- An older person with dementia living on their own.

How might these influence, help, or hinder your social work practice?

In my own research (Hughes 2011a, 2011b), I worked with a group of final-year social work students to explore the impact of social work education on their lives. In relation to the impact of life experiences on their practice, Terry explained how he had worked with a family where the mother had fled 'extreme domestic and sexual violence'. This had led him to reflect on his own childhood experiences in a violent family home. While this gave him insight, particularly into the impact of domestic violence on children, he explained how it had also led him to make an assumption.

Student perspective

> I made an assumption that she would be struggling more than she was, but I checked it out with other agencies and she is doing brilliantly, fantastically, really resilient. I made this assumption that things would fall apart. That really opened my eyes.

Terry's self-awareness and ability to critically reflect on the assessment he made in practice enabled him to identify how he had drawn on previous experiences to help him understand the woman's situation, but also to recognize how this had led him to assume a particular outcome. Recognizing this enabled him to change his practice by considering personal experiences, but by being open to other experiences too.

Assad, when discussing links between his own identity, life experiences and his practice, identified similarities, but also conflicts, between his religious and cultural beliefs and his social work values, which he wanted to balance.

Student perspective

> My values are shaped by my religion because I am Muslim. You have to respect everybody. If you do good things, good things happen to you. Treat others as you expect to be treated. There are so many differences. If you look at discrimination, if you are Muslim, you can't talk with gay people. Although you are allowed to work with women, they have a different role in society, so that is another challenge with the course. In my own culture, mental health and disability are like a big curse, so that's another thing. I challenge them.

Assad learned to balance these views by focusing on values shared by his religion and his chosen profession: in particular, *respect*. He extended this respect to all people, regardless of sexuality, disability and gender, and challenged others within his family and community on the need to do this. He achieved this balance through critical reflection, openness to the views of others, and through awareness of how his beliefs and values could both help and hinder his social work practice.

Vicky was able to identify how an experience for her had positively informed her practice. She explained how, in her personal life, she had become involved with someone who turned out to be violent. As a result she had sought police intervention.

***

Student perspective

On my placement I started working with someone who had suffered domestic violence from her husband for 12 years, and I thought, 'gosh' – I had the tiniest experience, literally a week of feeling quite scared, and then I sorted it out, and she's lived with that for years. While I look back and think I was a bit naive, it was a good experience to have because I've learned so much from it, and I was able to help her because the other worker said she hadn't known all that I had. Because I had personal experience, I was able to deal with it better.

***

Vicky drew on her personal experience to consider the severity of the situation for the woman she was working with. She also drew on formal knowledge of the legal system and the support available gained through her personal experiences. Through reflection and awareness of self, she recognized that she needed to keep her own experiences separate and focus on the needs and experiences of the woman she was working with, and not to assume that their experiences were similar.

Developing this self-awareness enables you to identify the aspects of your life experiences you can draw on to help you develop as a competent practitioner. It can provide you with the insight, knowledge and skills required to respond to particular situations and needs.

Personal experiences can also negatively affect or influence your judgements and assessments. For example, when seeking to understand someone's experiences, you may assume that they will be like your own. This can also influence your judgements when considering subjective terms such as what is 'appropriate care', 'good enough parenting', or 'appropriate risk-taking'. It is likely that you will draw on your own values and beliefs regarding parenting, or the acceptability of particular behaviours within your culture. So it is essential, as a social worker, to understand these influences and consider how else you can view a particular situation and what other knowledge you can draw on to make a balanced judgement. It is also an essential part of competent practice that you develop resilience given the difficult experiences you may encounter, but also the resonance this may have for you. This will be explored later in this chapter.

Use of self in the learning process

As we have mentioned, one way of developing self-awareness and recognizing the impact of your beliefs, values and experiences on your practice is though critical reflection and analysis. The College of Social Work (TCSW 2012a), when exploring the expectations of this within the capabilities, identify it as being able to 'identify, distinguish, evaluate and integrate multiple sources of knowledge and evidence'.

Critical reflection and analysis in social work education

Social workers require the skills to make sense of and learn from their experiences and developing knowledge, and to make improvements to their practice as a result. In Chapter 5, we discussed the requirements for you to develop a broad knowledge base which can be applied to different service users, situations and settings. Critical reflection on your use of self is a way of ensuring this.

Mezirow et al. (1990: 1) identify reflection as enabling 'us to correct distortions in our beliefs and errors in problem-solving'. It involves asking questions of ourselves, our judgements, and our practice. Mezirow's view was that we make sense of a situation by interpreting it, and that interpretation is based on prior experiences, beliefs, assumptions and what we expect to happen. This is a widely held view in adult learning, which recognizes that we try and make sense of new information and experiences by relating it to what we already know. When making an assessment of someone's parenting, for example, we are likely to relate this to our own experiences of being a parent, of our relationship with our own parents, or our previous practice or work experience. This is likely to influence our views on what is 'good enough' parenting. Given this process of making sense of a situation based on our current knowledge and previous experience, it is essential that we recognize what our previous experience, beliefs and values are, and how they will inform our assessments and decisions in practice. While they may give you insight, to what extent is your view biased? Looking back at activities 6.2 and 6.3, how did your background influence your judgement of whether the scenario was acceptable or not? How might this affect your view of the person?

Mezirow (1990) defined critical reflection as involving 'a critique of the presuppositions on which our beliefs have been built' (1990: 1). This involves not only questioning what your knowledge, values and beliefs are, and how they may influence your practice, but also asking why you think that. It involves challenging your own values, beliefs and behaviour, and questioning whether there is wider evidence to support your view or belief.

Social work education seeks to enable you to develop skills in critical analysis and reflection in order to meet the value requirements of the profession, and be able to adapt your practice to different situations and contexts to achieve the best outcomes for those involved. This will need to be evidenced within your practice and within your portfolio.

In relation to critical reflection and the use of self, you are encouraged to reflect on how your own experiences, views and beliefs have positively or negatively influenced your decisions and judgements, and to consider the implications on the outcome for the person. As Chow et al. (2011: 143) identify, students are encouraged to engage in a dual process. Reflective people 'use their personal experience to understand and critique the knowledge that is introduced to them. And, they appraise and make sense of their personal experience using that knowledge'.

In Chapter 5, there was an activity to help you recognize what you base your knowledge of a particular context, issue or community on. This sought to establish that much of your knowledge is based on what you know from your upbringing, personal experiences, and the views of those around you. The reflective process involves the use of self and of experiential learning to 'make sense' of situations and events in both professional and personal contexts, and to draw on a wider range of evidence and knowledge to reflect, analyse, challenge or support these views.

While the aim of critical reflection is to achieve effective practice and better outcomes for those involved, there is a risk of conflict if you find yourself within practice learning environments which are dominated by procedures which seem to restrict this. It can be difficult to be the social worker you want to be when constrained by targets, deadlines, case recording, eligibility criteria, and limited funding and resources. This concern was raised by Munro (2011) when criticizing a system based on following rules at the expense of exercising professional expertise and judgement. Mackay and Woodward (2010) identified that this can lead to disillusionment among students and practitioners. Engaging in critical reflection can be a means of seeking ways to challenge systems in the best interest of service users and carers, but also to work creatively within them. The College of Social Work (TCSW 2012a) suggest that critical thinking should be augmented by creativity and curiosity. Failing to do this can inhibit your own practice and the outcomes for those involved. In evidencing competent practice within your portfolio, it is important to demonstrate this level of critical thinking and creativity within your practice.

Personal and professional development

One way of demonstrating your understanding of your use of self, your developing self-awareness, and your skills in critical reflection and analysis, is to identify your personal and professional journey – how you have developed. It is easy as a student, experiencing the pressures of placement and of being continually assessed, to lose sight of your achievements along the way. The following activity helps you to consider what your development has been.

Activity 6.5: What do you know now that you didn't know then?

Completion of this activity involves thinking back to your starting point. You may want to draw on your reflective diary or log, or feedback from others.

- Describe yourself at the start of your placement. What were your views and initial thoughts of the service user group and your ability to work within this area of practice?
- What has changed?

Students within my own research study (Hughes 2012) identified a number of areas where they felt they had changed or developed. This was largely as a result of becoming more self-aware, or more aware of other views, perspectives and areas of knowledge.

Jessica explained that the knowledge and experience she gained from her social work education had made her more confident to challenge injustice with people in both her personal and professional life. Assad said he learned to speak up more. Linda reflected on how she had changed:

Student perspective

The social work degree probably affects how I interact with individuals. Sometimes I think of some of the things I might have said or done, and I cringe a little bit. Like when I thought I'm right about something, and in part that might be down to age, but maybe not. Maybe I was less tolerant then. I thought I was being open-minded but I wasn't. That's about sitting and reflecting back on things.

Taking the time to reflect back on these changes is a useful part of your own learning and development, and can be shared within your portfolio to show how you have become more self-aware and how you are consciously reflecting on the impact of your learning and development on your practice.

Activity 6.6: Reflecting on your personal and professional development

Go back to your personal profile in Activity 6.2 and your reflections in Activities 6.3 and 6.4. What aspects have been affected by your social work education?

Have your views changed? Have you become more aware of particular aspects of your identity or self, or how they may influence your practice?

In this chapter so far, we have considered why it is important to reflect on the use of self within your practice. We have considered how personal qualities, experiences, views and values have a significant impact on how we make sense of situations we are presented with, and how we make judgements and assessments. The activities and examples presented so far have sought to enable you to consider your own identity and beliefs, how these may impact on your practice, as well as recognizing your learning and development throughout your social work education. Many of the examples lead us to consider another area of developing social work practice where use of self is important. This is in relation to your development as an anti-oppressive practitioner.

Anti-oppressive practice

It is important to consider your own social status and identity when considering the issues relating to power and oppression. Social work education can be effective in enabling you to recognize oppression at different levels, and evaluate your own strategies in challenging oppression within social work practice and the lives of those you encounter. Recognizing your own power and social status is the first step to achieving this. Your personal profile completed within this chapter, and your reflections on it, can be used to explore the development of your anti-oppressive practice in terms of acknowledging your power and social status, but also the judgements and assumptions your beliefs, values and life experiences can lead you to make.

Visibility of self within your portfolio (reflective writing)

Having established the importance of acknowledging and reflecting on your use of self in your practice, we need to consider how this can be demonstrated within your portfolio. In social work education, this is commonly demonstrated through the use of supervision and through critically reflective and analytical written work. Requirements vary from programme to programme, but evidence may include assignments, reflective logs, presentations, critical incident analyses, and evaluations of direct observations of practice. Reflection involves looking back on practice, asking questions of what happened, making sense of what happened, and analysing what you have learned. For reflection and analysis to be meaningful, you need to make changes to your future practice as a result. There are many models of reflection that can facilitate this process and help you consider different stages of a reflective cycle.

Borton (1970, cited in Dundon 2012) suggested the model of 'What?, So what?, and Now what?'

What?

Involves providing a detailed description of the event, such as background, context, what happened, what I did, what I said, what others said.

So what?

Involves breaking down, analysing, and asking questions of what happened: How did I feel? How do I feel now? What was good? What wasn't so good? What were my views based on? Why did I think that? Why did it happen? What did others there think? What does the person I'm discussing it with think about it? How can I use wider knowledge sources, such as literature and research, to help me understand what happened?

Now what?

Involves consideration of what you can do in the future as a result of your learning: What have I learned? What should I do about it? Do I need to respond differently next time? What do I need to know to change things? What are my options? What strategies can I find through wider reading and research to enhance my practice?

Activity 6.7: What?, So what?, and Now what?

Using these questions, reflect back on a particular piece of practice. It could be an example of something that went well, or something that you feel could have been better.

It can be common for students when writing about practice to focus predominantly on the descriptive stage (What?). While this enables you, and someone assessing your practice, to see what you did, it shows little of the thinking behind your practice. Evidencing your use of self, and your ability to critically reflect and analyse your practice, demonstrates your understanding, your awareness, and your knowledge. It shows that you are able to adapt your practice when faced with different situations, and as your knowledge, skills and experience develops. Demonstrating this in your portfolio involves focusing on the analysis and future planning stages of reflection in addition to describing what you did.

In Chapter 5, a model is provided to show the links that can be explored between use of self, your developing knowledge, practice environment, and the service user group you are working with. Critical reflection and analysis of these component parts, and the links between them, can lead to an increased knowledge, awareness and understanding which can enhance the effectiveness of your practice. By the end of the final placement the expectations within the PCF are for you to be able to make these links, to apply a broad knowledge base to a range of settings and service user groups, and to recognize and manage the ethical dilemmas that these present. Drawing on models of reflection to facilitate this process can enable you to learn from your previous experiences and adapt this effectively to new situations and dilemmas. Models of reflection and reflecting within supervision, or with the support of others, can help you to consider questions that you had not thought to ask. Including these reflections within your portfolio provides evidence of your capabilities and your evidence-based practice.

Resilience

A final area where the use of self is important in developing as a social worker is in the development of resilience. In recognition of the demands of the profession, the Social Work Task Force (2009: 17) identified resilience as an essential quality in social work students. Social work practice and social work education can be stressful. The emphasis made in this chapter on personal qualities, and the need for you to challenge your beliefs, values and knowledge, can feel unsettling as it changes the way you view the world. Situations you encounter within your practice, and issues explored within university-based learning, can also be distressing, and in some cases may have personal resonance for you given your previous experiences. Recognizing the use of self in your practice, and developing self-awareness, can also enable you to identify and respond to the impact of stress and stressful situations and to develop strategies for minimizing this impact. The final activity for this chapter seeks to enable you to consider what situations you might find stressful, and to identify strategies for managing stress and stressful situations as a student and in your future career.

Activity 6.8: Managing stress and stressful situations

Consider the following scenarios. How might you react?

- You have observed or listened to a service user share their personal experiences and find what they have disclosed very upsetting. What they have been through is horrendous. You are amazed at their resilience, but left feeling very upset at what you have heard.
- You have received feedback from a colleague which you perceive as negative.
- You are about to speak in front of a large group of people. This may be something you are attending as part of your placement, such as a training event, case conference, court, or team meeting. This means a lot to you and you don't want to mess it up.

What strategies could you use to minimize the negative impact of stress in these situations?

Ask those around you (colleagues, peers, family, friends) for their top tips on managing stress and stressful situations. Identify what would work for you.

How could you demonstrate your resilience and professional development within your portfolio?

When being assessed, you may find it difficult to be open about the impact of stress, a lack of resilience, mistakes made, or concerns you have in your abilities. Competent practice, however, is about acknowledging areas in need of development in order to identify solutions or responses. Reflecting on strategies to develop resilience within your portfolio demonstrates professionalism and a commitment and openness to ongoing learning and development, and will provide you with skills and strategies for managing the demands of the profession throughout your career.

Key learning points

- How you practice is as important to what you practice.
- Self-awareness leads to improved critical reflection, analysis and practice.
- Recognition of your own identity and social status is fundamental to developing as an anti-oppressive practitioner.
- Awareness of self can enable you to develop strategies for improving your resilience.

7 Meaningful service user and carer involvement in student placements

Gill Calvin Thomas

Introduction

This chapter explores how service users and carers can be meaningfully involved in practice education and, in turn, how you should evidence their involvement within your placement portfolio. Throughout the chapter we use the generic term 'service user', which refers to both service users and carers, as being people who use services and who are experts by experience. Links will be made throughout to the Professional Capabilities Framework (PCF) (TCSW 2012b) focusing on the 'end of first placement' level.

The chapter begins by setting out some of the background to service user involvement in social work education. It continues with the underlying principles of why and how you can meaningfully involve service users in your practice placements. Pre-placement preparation, and the process of drawing up the practice learning agreement, are discussed, and information given to enable you to reflect on your own experience.

Different practice contexts are acknowledged, and examples of meaningful service user involvement within practice learning opportunities are put forward. The value of service user involvement in all the processes of the practice placement is reflected on, from induction through to the final review. Reflective activities and models are offered to help you think how you will integrate service user perspectives within your portfolio.

As in previous chapters, perspectives from students, service users and practice educators are presented, evidencing the richness of learning that service user involvement in practice learning can bring to you in your practice placement.

Lastly, key learning and themes are introduced, and a student action plan proposed.

By the end of the chapter you will be able to:

- Apply the principles and ideas within this chapter to your practice placement.
- Recognize the relevance and importance of service user involvement in your placement.
- Identify how you can evidence service user perspectives and the impact of service user involvement on your learning within your portfolio.

Background to user involvement in social work education

It has long been recognized that the involvement of service users in social work education would be a valuable way of raising standards in social care (Branfield 2009). Branfield (2007), in the 'Shaping our Lives' project, set out to develop strategies to support the participation of service users in social work education. A participant in the project explained: 'It is very important that we are heard and universities recognize that we are experts by experience.'

Shaping our Lives sees the term 'service user' as active and positive. However, the term may also represent:

- An unequal and oppressive relationship with the state and society as a whole.
- An entitlement to receive welfare services which may set service users apart from other people, and make them appear inferior.
- A wide range of people with diverse experiences who could have a forceful voice in improving and controlling the kind of services they are given.

On the other hand, the term 'service user' could be seen to restrict identity, giving the impression that service users are passive recipients of services, and ignoring the experiences and strengths that make service users who they are. It could also suggest that changing terminology would be beneficial. However, service users believe that the best way to challenge those negative perceptions is for them to 'tell it as it is' (SCIE 2009).

With this in mind, universities have come some way in involving user groups in social work degree programmes – for example, including service users in the design and management of programmes, interviewing and teaching. Surprisingly, however, there is little evidence of user involvement in social work placements (Sadd 2011). Participants in the SCIE project, Developing User Involvement in Social Work Education (SCIE 2009), clearly felt that service users should be involved in all aspects of social work education, and that it 'was an essential component of good practice'. Therefore, in this chapter we will argue and provide evidence – from service user, student and practice educator experiences – that service user involvement in student placements is vital to student learning and assessment, and that the service user perspective should be a major element in the practice portfolio.

Now listen to the voice of a service user who has been involved within the higher education institute (HEI) setting who is talking about the impact and benefit to service users being involved in practice education.

A service user perspective

Payment for what we do is about more than money. It is about being respected for our status. Service users who want to be involved in practice education need to have a passion and to understand what is involved.

The service user can be using the service, or may have come out of the service. They can be involved at different levels.

The spin-off for service users is that they can use their new skills and confidence to go on to educating the public in their community. This is needed because people in the community never think it will happen to them.

The problem is there is so much stereotyping and negative reporting in the media. If a service user is doing well and doing good work out there in the community, it won't hit the headlines; you have to be a celebrity for that to happen. For a service user it would have to be really sensational!

There is a sense from the above narrative that service users find their involvement with practice education valuable, not just in terms of enabling students, but valuable for them even outside of practice education.

The challenge has been in creating systems whereby students can involve service users in a meaningful way in their placements. At the most basic level, most social work programmes ask students to produce written feedback from service users. Although we have used the word 'basic', in asking for and receiving meaningful feedback about your practice, it may be more complicated than you think. Most placement agencies ask for feedback about their services, but this is not the same thing.

Activity 7.1: Asking for feedback

Take a few minutes to think about the following questions:

- Why do you think agencies ask for feedback about their services?
- What would be different about you asking for feedback as a student social worker?

Note down your answers. We will return to written feedback later in this chapter, offering a service user perspective.

Developing meaningful involvement of service users in practice

Sadd (2011) suggested that social work programmes should begin to consider how service users could be involved in social work placements, and offered the 'hub and spoke' model (2009).

The model in Figure 7.1 has a 'hub' at its centre. Sadd (2011) suggests that the service user is central to the hub, and can be involved in all the 'spokes'. We would add that while you are in placement the hub should contain you, as the student, as well as the service user/ users. However, not all service users who contribute to your learning would want to be part of the 'hub', and those who are would primarily choose to be, and would receive support to attain that role, within your practice education.

From reading previous chapters you will have gained an understanding that, as a student, you are not a passive recipient in your placement. You will be taking an active role in your own learning and assessment. In addition, during placement you will be working with your practice educator, and you may also have an on-site placement supervisor/work-based supervisor. This partnership will have been set up primarily to support, teach and assess you while you are undertaking practice learning. Throughout this chapter we refer to this 'extended hub' as the practice learning support team.

Practice learning offers you an opportunity to develop your evidence-based practice in accordance with the PCF. Utilizing some of the ideas from the model above, we will now begin to focus on how people who use services can contribute to your learning and assessment. Each section will link with the PCF and will offer ideas, reflective activities and models that will enable you to provide evidence of your learning in practice.

Starting out: Asking the age-old questions, what, who, when, why, where and how?

In order to transfer learning into your portfolio you have to start out in your placement with ideas of how you might want to involve service users in your education. In other words, we

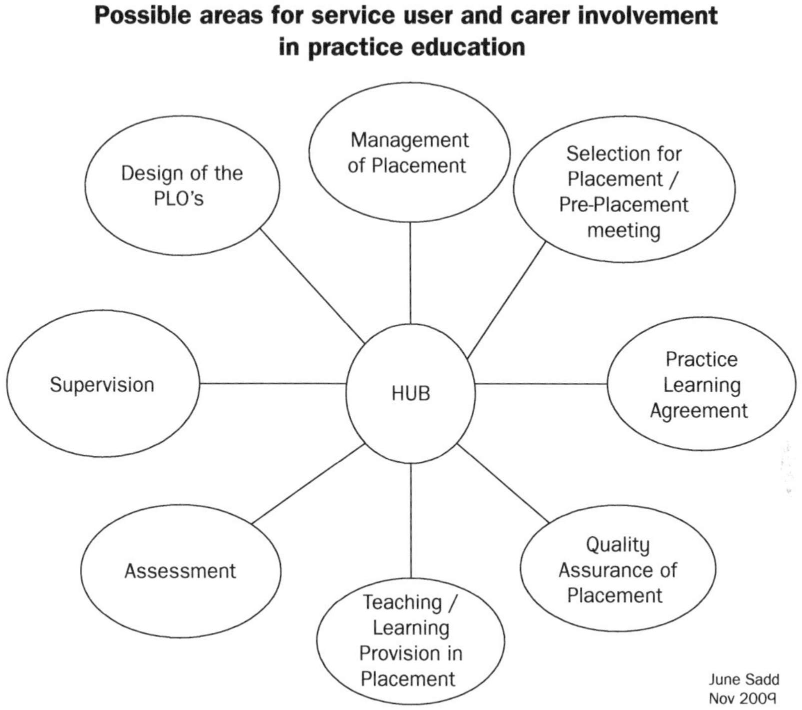

**Possible areas for service user and carer involvement
in practice education**

Figure 7.1 Areas for Service User and Carer Involvement in Practice Education

Source: Bournemouth University Social Work Practice Learning Handbook, 2009. Reproduced with permission.

need to briefly explore the process of meaningful involvement before identifying how that learning might be evidenced in your portfolio.

What?

In the first instance as a learner you must find out what process there may be in place to involve service users in practice in your particular programme. Following on from there, you may wish to make use of some or all of the ideas provided in this chapter to enhance your learning. This must be in negotiation with your practice learning support team.

Who?

Primarily, you, your practice learning support team, and people who use services or have been the recipient of services in your placement agency.

When?

Ideally the focus on service user involvement should begin when preparing for placement. Sadd (2011) suggests that service users can be present at the pre-placement meeting and at the practice learning agreement meeting. In order to provide this degree of service user involvement, the agency and your learning support team would be involved in prior forward planning.

Why?

SCIE (2009) found that service users thought their involvement in social work education was often tokenistic and just a way to 'tick a box'. The following extract from the SCIE's report goes some way to helping us to reflect on the importance of service user involvement in all contexts in social work education. 'I think, by being genuine, by telling our own stories and other people's stories and showing where mistakes have been made, what has helped us most and what has not helped us. This will give an idea of what it's like to be on the receiving end, to look at things from a different angle.'

In addition, the PCF makes it very clear, in terms of values and ethics, that students must:

- Elicit and respect the needs and views of service users and carers and, with support, promote their participation in decision-making, wherever possible.
- Inform practice through respectful partnership work with service users, carers and professionals.

Where?

In both your practice learning placements.

How?

Drawing on the model above, with a focus on learning opportunities, teaching and learning, supervision and assessment.

Preparation

Before your placement even begins – that is, during your preparation for practice and your pre-placement visit – you may have reflected on your learning style and your learning needs in the placement. You will have met your practice educator. You may have discussed and debated how service users will be involved in your placement, including the induction to your placement (see *Action planning* at the end of this chapter). You may have sought out literature and online resources to help you explore service user perspectives.

The practice learning agreement

Usually the first formal process in your placement is the meeting to set out the practice learning arrangements – this is the document commonly referred to as the 'practice learning agreement'.

The agreement will set out the process of your placement. It will focus on your learning and the support you need to enable you to learn best. Much of your learning will arise from the direct work you will be doing with service users.

Your learning needs will be discussed, and learning opportunities will be suggested to meet those needs. It is at this point that you may wish to discuss how involving service users will enrich your learning opportunities. Indeed, you and your learning support team may have been proactive and identified a service user from the agency who will be willing to mentor you and offer their ideas about learning opportunities. The most important point here is for you to take a proactive part in your practice learning agreement in terms of involving service users in your learning, in order for you to shape and own your learning.

Activity 7.2: Your learning agreement

Take a few minutes now to reflect and make a note of the important issues for you:

- Why do you think it is important for you to be an active participant in your practice learning agreement?
- How are you going to prepare for your learning agreement?
- What is the rationale for involving service users in your placement learning?

Practice contexts

Practice contexts are varied. Some placements may lend themselves immediately to service user involvement. For example, there could be placements in day resources, residential units, service user-led organizations, family centres, or housing provisions. In these contexts, work can be longer term, and service user involvement can be negotiated and planned in advance.

Contexts where work with service users is shorter term may be difficult to plan in advance, but not impossible, as you will see below. In some placements, service users may be involuntary – for example, in child protection. However, your practice educator may, for example, be able to arrange for you to talk with service users who have been subject to child protection processes in their past.

Each new placement is an exciting possibility for new learning. When you first know where your placement is, you may feel daunted. We would suggest that you research all you can about the service user group you will be working with. This should give you ideas, from the very beginning, of how you might involve service users in your education.

The following examples show how students from a university have either been given opportunities or have organized opportunities for service user involvement at the beginning of their placements.

Examples of service user involvement in different contexts

A residential unit for looked-after children – the idea was to engage as many of the young people as wanted to be involved in thinking about the characteristics they would like to see in a social worker (this may be a pictorial representation). Following this, the young people would give feedback to the student on how they were developing their skills. They also identified specific areas for learning for the student.

In an advocacy setting and a residential unit within a specialist school, students worked in partnership with young people with learning disabilities. The young people taught the students particular communication skills, including Makaton.

In a local authority child-safeguarding team, the practice educator arranged for students to visit families who had been through child protection procedures and who were willing to talk about their experiences.

In a family centre setting, a service user agreed that an interaction with himself and the student could be recorded so that he could watch the interaction again with the student and give the student live feedback.

In a housing provision, a service user came to part of the student's supervision session so that she could help the student reflect on their practice and give feedback. The same service user took the student through the health and safety provision within the house.

In a day centre provision service, users were prepared to take the student around all the group activities, and thereafter acted as mentors to the student providing valuable insights and support for the student.

In a variety of settings, service users have become part of the learning support team and taken part in reviews of the student's progress, contributing live feedback, and helping students reflect on how they will take their learning forward.

Now go back to the reflective notes you made about the important issues for you in service user involvement – you may be able to reflect in more depth now if you think about the context of your placement and the sorts of opportunities that may be available.

It can be seen from the few examples above that service user involvement in your placement could be discussed with your practice educator at the pre-placement meeting, and agreed in your practice learning agreement, if you agree that specific involvement will be beneficial for your learning needs and will help you evidence practice requirements.

Induction

It is important for you to begin your portfolio early on in the placement. Indeed you may already have your practice learning agreement drafted and ready for signatures. You will be undertaking your induction to the agency. An essential part of that induction will be meeting the people who use the service.

Service users can form an important part of your induction. Individual service users could have been asked beforehand by your practice educator or placement supervisor if they would talk to you about their experiences. You may also ask the service users you meet in the placement, explaining that you are a student in learning and would like to hear what it is like to be a service user. This is the beginning of meaningful service user involvement as service users 'tell it as it is' (SCIE 2009).

Activity 7.3: Service users

Reflect, and make some brief notes, on the following questions:

- How would you prepare to meet with service users?
- What sort of questions do you want to ask?
- What do you want to find out about the expectations service users have of you as a student in learning?
- How are you going to enable service users to 'tell it as it is'? How will you convey that you will value negative comments as well as positive ones?
- How are you going to use the knowledge you gain to develop your learning?

The learning log

Your programme may require you to keep a learning log or a diary of your learning. A learning log is an important element of your learning and may form part of your portfolio. During your induction, the learning log can include:

- The knowledge you are gaining about the placement and the community it serves.
- What you are learning about yourself in a new working environment.
- The insights you are gaining from engaging with the people who work in the service and the people who use the service.

Now go back to the notes you made above. Make some further notes about how you would record what you have learned, and how you will reflect on the insights you have gained about service user experiences, using your learning log. For example, reflect on how you talked about your student role and how you felt about negative comments.

Service user perspective

Listening to the service user will help the student examine their own personal values, unlearning what they may already have been taught.

Listening to, and trying to make sense of service user experiences will be a rich seam of analysis for you in your learning log. You may be able to use extracts from the log in your portfolio – for example, in analyses of practice, in which you can demonstrate your learning. Another useful way of using extracts from the log will be in your supervision sessions with your practice educator who will help you reflect on your values and the assumptions you may unconsciously make.

Supervision

Supervision is a key part of your learning. Workplace supervision is paramount to ensuring service users are being provided with appropriate services. You will also receive practice teaching in which your practice educator will help you develop and learn from your experiences. (To read more about supervision and practice teaching, please refer to Chapter 4.) Sadd (2011) suggests that supervision can be one of the 'spokes' in her model, and that service users can transfer valuable insights from their perspective into practice. She adds that service user involvement in supervision can feel threatening to the professional role. On the other hand, supervision can benefit from service user expertise – for example, on social work values, relationship-based work practice, as well as anti-oppressive and anti-discriminatory practice.

So including service users in supervision is an aspect requiring discussion and careful preparation with your practice educator and the service user themselves. However, from student and service user reflections on practice in supervision, we believe including service users in supervision can be priceless in providing those important 'light bulb' moments for you. Service users must be willing, and understand their role in your learning. It also calls for you to be prepared for, and open to, honest and constructive feedback on your practice (see Chapter 4). Feedback will be recorded and will form part of the assessment of your progression within your portfolio.

Example from practice

In a housing provision, a service user agreed to act as a mentor to the student. Having worked closely with the student the mentor then joined part of the student's workplace supervision. It was agreed that confidentiality would be maintained, and that supervision during that time focused on the mentor's engagement with the student.

The mentor was able to give constructive feedback to the student and map how the student developed in their practice. The feedback from the mentor was included in the student's portfolio.

The service user later commented that 'it was like a key working session the other way around', and that being part of the student experience helped the student and 'made me feel worthwhile'.

Observation of practice

It is a requirement of the degree that students are directly observed in practice. There are several models of observation you can refer to, such as the York Model (2011). Observations will generally involve direct work with a service user/users, and informed consent must be obtained.

Observation is a learning tool. It gives you, as the student, an opportunity to evidence your professional development and knowledge. And it gives the practice educator an opportunity to observe your professional development and knowledge, and offer you constructive criticism.

Having your practice observed also gives service users an opportunity to provide feedback about your practice. Observation of practice is therefore an opportunity for you to plan for meaningful involvement of the service user in your observation, if it is appropriate. This goes some way towards the quality assurance 'spoke' in the model proposed by Sadd (2011).

You should ensure that you follow the guidance in your programme's practice handbook. In addition, you can discuss whether it is appropriate to involve service users in a more meaningful way with your practice educator. By including the service user in your planning and reflection, you and service user can have more control over the experience. You can agree the sort of feedback that would be most useful for your learning with the service user – for example, feedback on communication skills.

Activity 7.4: Planning your observed practice

You are planning for your observed practice. You have identified a service user who has agreed that your practice educator can observe you working with them. You are reflecting on how you can ask the service user for feedback. You have worked with the service user once before, but it is a short-term piece of work. Now put yourself in the service user's shoes and make some notes on how you think a service user might feel being asked to give feedback following an observed practice session.

- How would you feel about being asked for feedback following an observed practice?
- Would you want the student present?
- Would you want to know what questions were going to be asked beforehand?
- Would you want to fill in a form rather than openly discuss with the practice educator, who you may never have met before?
- Would you feel worried about the responsibility of giving feeding back about the student? This could have an impact on whether they pass or fail!

Would you be concerned that it may affect the service you receive in the future?

At the beginning of this chapter we suggested that, at the most basic level, programmes can ask students to produce written feedback from service users. Having reflected on the activity above, how difficult might it be to elicit honest and constructive feedback – feedback that is meaningful and useful to inform your learning?

A student perspective

I did design some feedback forms to help me develop my practice, but mostly what I got was ticks. I think the majority of people say what they think you want to hear. They want to please the person because they want to be liked.

I worked with some groups, and found that just using Post-it notes was more honest. I gave them out and asked the group to write a word, sentence, or make a suggestion just to show what they felt. One person wrote a rude word. I asked him if he had really thought that, and he told me that he just liked writing the word, and actually the group was great!

We need to ask the question: Is there another way of using observed practice as a learning tool in which meaningful service user feedback becomes accepted practice?

Reflection, in practice, is a skill that has already been explored in Chapters 3 and 5. The model set out below (Table 7.1) builds on established models of reflection – for example, the model requires reflection before action (Greenwood 1998), reflection in action (Schon 1996; Kolb 1984), and reflection following the action (Gibbs 1988, Boud and Walker 1998). At the beginning of this chapter it was suggested that service users are experts by experience (Shaping our Lives 2007). The proposed model for planning and reflecting on your observed practice therefore asks for a more integrated approach in gaining meaningful feedback. You, as the student, would be required to plan the interaction and include the service user in your planning. This sort of approach reflects the inclusive philosophy of the exchange model of assessment in which service users are seen as experts and contributors to the assessment and planning process (Milner and O'Byrne 2002).

Planning, or reflection before action, enables you to think through what it is you are being tasked to do, what you intend to do, and how you intend to do it. It also enables you to think through to the outcome. But that does not mean to say that you have to stick rigidly to your plan. You should also plan to be flexible in order to meet the needs of the service user.

Table 7.1 Meaningful Service User Involvement – A model for planning and reflecting on observed practice (currently inside the box)

Meaningful service user involvement: A model for planning and reflecting on observed practice.
Reflection before action: Reflecting on the task, and utilizing service user/carer feedback.
The task: What does the service user/carer want to achieve? What do I want to achieve?
- Identify and agree the task.
- Identify relevant knowledge and skills that will underpin your practice.
- Acknowledge core values – reflect on anti-oppressive practice.
- Recognize feelings – positive and negative.
- Reflect on assumptions already held.

Reflecting on action: The experience. Personal reflection.
- How do I feel about the experience now?
- How do I feel about the outcome of the experience?
- How do I feel about the power invested in my role and my own impact?
- Have I reflected on the goals before action been achieved? Did the goals change as part of the process, and did I adapt to those changes?
- Can I be open about what I might have done differently, with hindsight?

Evaluating the experience. Critical analysis. Working with supervisor and service user/carer.
- How does the service user/carer feel following the interaction?
- How relevant was my knowledge – was I able to meet the service user/carers' needs adequately?
- Recognizing the limits of my knowledge and understanding – what have I learned?
- How flexible was I in practice?
- Did I explore alternatives?
- Was I creative in practice?
- What have I evidenced in practice?

Action planning
- Recognize and act on my own learning needs in response to practice and practice feedback.
- What do I need to learn now?
- Who, and what, will help me learn?

Working in partnership with a service user, using the model above, would elicit meaningful feedback. It does, however, require you as the student to plan for the observation very carefully, to work with the service user beforehand, and prepare them for a reflection after the experience. The reflection would take place at a time of their choosing.

It must be acknowledged that it is not always possible to set observations up so carefully. However, where service users are meaningfully involved, it can redress the power differential and enable the service user to feel part of student learning.

Activity 7.5: Learning from observed practice

You have already been observed in practice. Take a few minutes to think about the following questions:

- How could this model have helped you in planning your observed practice?
- What might you have done differently if you had used the model?
- What have you learned having reflected on the model?
- Would you use the model next time, and if so why?

Observed practice

Written reflection on observed practice forms an important part of your portfolio. It provides live evidence of your professional development in practice. The observed practice can meet many of the competences within the PCF. The written reflection, which including meaningful service involvement in your practice, will evidence values, knowledge and skills. For instance: We acknowledged that it is not always possible or appropriate to include service users in planning and reflecting on practice. The service user may be more comfortable with the idea of providing feedback in a written form. The question this poses is how to design a feedback form that gives an opportunity for a service user to 'tell it as it is', and offer you constructive feedback. The following ideas are from a practice educator who has worked extensively with our programme.

A practice educator perspective

My student is in a voluntary placement working with young people. She started with the premise: 'What can the young people teach me about being a social worker?' We discussed starting a mini project that would last through the placement. The student had picked up on ideas about the child's journey from the Munro Report, adapted one form from the report, and designed one herself from scratch, basically to ask: 'What is a good social worker, and what is a bad one?' The young people were able to use words or drawings.

We discussed how the student needed to pick the right time, and that the process should meet the young people's needs as well as the students.

So the student picked young people who were a little further down the line, who were not in crisis. Generally, it was the young people who were looked-after children.

What the student found was that it was empowering for the young people, and they enjoyed the process. The student asked: 'What can you teach me? What things should I avoid?' The student has also been working with young carer groups, and plans to do a short session with them asking the same sorts of questions.

In terms of my assessment of the student, it has been very helpful. The student has realized that there are different ways of doing things. For example, just something small – like a young person saying that instead of sitting in a room with the social worker, they would prefer to go for a walk. It has helped me to see how the student has taken on and made connections with young people's perspectives. And it has certainly helped in the reflective process.

During supervision the student critically reflected on why one little girl did not want to say anything bad. We were able to unpick this and have a good discussion. I have been able to assess how and what the student has learned, and how she has developed her practice.

I have learned through working with my student, and found it very interesting. It is good to listen and to remember that small things make such a difference to practice – for example, understanding how anxious young people become when their social worker is late. As a practitioner, you can get caught up in practice and forget how important these things are.

I think working with service users in this way is far better than just asking for feedback. Getting feedback does not necessarily teach you, whereas what my student has been doing has. It is much better to go with the premise, 'What can you teach me and what can I learn?'

I have realized, from working with other programmes, how little importance other students put on service user involvement, and I think it is a missed learning opportunity. I also think that it helps assess a student's value base about how much they respect service user's views and whether they believe they have something to offer them in the learning process.

As a practitioner, working in a statutory setting, I think it may be easier to use meaningful service user involvement in an agency which is not an enforcement service. It will be harder to work with young people who are not so engaged. However, I think I can adapt this for my own practice too.

Now read Lucy's narrative and reflect on what she has learned:

A student perspective

Part of what I had to do for placement was write 500 words to attach to my learning agreement on how I would meaningfully involve service users in my practice education, so I had to think about what would be the best way for me to learn. I researched on the internet and, in my search for gaining feedback from young people, came up with the Munro Report.

My experience of previously working with families helped me to understand that families and young people criticize social workers for being late, not giving them enough time, and being too busy. I want to always be aware of that.

I discussed designing a form based on the example in the Munro Report with my practice educator (Figure 7.2). When she looked at the form she thought that the scaling was confusing, so I amended it. I also designed another form myself where children could write or draw in boxes (Figure 7.3). I wanted to learn from the children and young people what they felt would make a good social worker. I thought I might already know, but was aware that that might not be so. I wanted the children and young people to take the lead; I wanted it to be child-friendly and age appropriate. I am going to adapt what I have been doing to work with a young carer's group.

I was aware that not all the children I was working with would want to fill in the form, particularly if they were still at a crisis stage. When I had worked with a child for a period of time, I was able to explain what I was doing and why. I had to be sensitive, assessing whether a child was ready.

It was interesting working with one child who did not want to fill out the box asking what was not so good. It enabled me to reflect on why. It may be that I didn't explain well enough that it was for me to learn from her. She may have felt fearful.

Lots of children enjoyed drawing in the boxes. Others wrote things like, 'kind and helped us when . . .', 'good social worker = happy, not so good = grumpy'. This helped me to reflect about body language and how some social workers might indeed come over as looking 'grumpy', although might not mean to. Another comment that helped me learn was, 'ignores my comments'. This has reinforced to me that I must be aware and actively listen.

I've noticed that young people like being asked; I think it gives them some power. For example, when they are in crisis it may feel very negative for them, the whole idea of having to work with social services may feel negative, and so it is important to look at what is good. I have attended quite a few child protection conferences and have observed that parents sometimes express that they would rather their child be subject to a childcare plan because that is how they get support. Having spent time in my placement truly trying to understand service user perspectives has led me to believe that the support element of social care needs to come across more strongly. This message can get lost.

I have learned that a lot of children prefer to be seen at home or in their foster carer's home, rather than at school, because they don't like being taken out in front of the class and their friends. They often don't get told in advance what the visit is about by their social workers, so they worry that they are in trouble. On the other hand, some children do like being taken out, and like to go for a drink or a walk. I think understanding these different perspectives is so important to the young people, and something social workers should be mindful of when arranging visits.

Child protection conferences can be daunting. I supported two young people to attend a conference so they could discuss what they wanted. I then observed the social worker question those young people aggressively because they were presenting some different perspectives to what the social worker had understood. I think those young people will never go to a child conference again. That was the only time I have witnessed such a lack of understanding, but it taught me a lot. I always want to listen and be sensitive to what young people are saying.

My placement supervisor has been working with a year one group from my university, and I have been able to talk to them about what I have been doing here to help their learning. I have a presentation to do at the end of my placement, and I am going to prepare some handouts to share my new knowledge with my group. I now have a real passion for working with children; it's what I want to do when I graduate.

Lucy's forms – the first form is adapted from the Munro Report (2011):

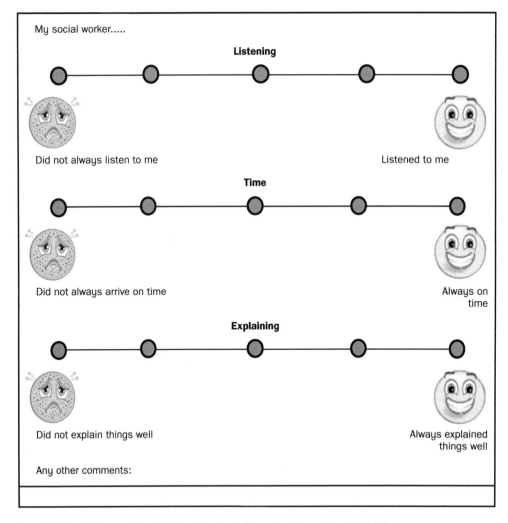

My social worker.....

Listening

Did not always listen to me   Listened to me

Time

Did not always arrive on time   Always on time

Explaining

Did not explain things well   Always explained things well

Any other comments:

Figure 7.2 Lucy's Forms – The first form is adapted from the Munro Report (2011)

Lucy designed the second form:

A good social worker is...

You can draw a picture or write here...

A bad social worker is...

You can draw a picture or write here...

Figure 7.3 Lucy's Form (designed by Lucy)

Activity 7.6: Your feedback form

Reflect on the service user group you are working with. Will you use a form? If so:

- How will you design your feedback form? Who will you ask?
- What format would your feedback form take?
- What do you want to learn about your practice? How will you ask the questions?
- What sort of language are you going to use?
- How will you use the feedback to inform future practice?

Critical reflection of practice

Supervision offers you a chance to regularly reflect with your practice educator on the work you are undertaking in practice (see Chapter 4). You may have included a service user as part of your supervision sessions. Similarly, direct observations of practice can also enable you to critically reflect, individually, with your practice educator and with a service user.

Direct observation of practice forms a major part of your portfolio. Meaningful service user involvement and feedback on the direct observation should be an integral element within the documentation in the portfolio.

It is not so easy to map how learning in supervision forms an integral element of the portfolio, unless your programme asks for supervision notes to be included. As supervision is a fundamental building block of your placement, it is advantageous to evidence the development of your learning in supervision within your portfolio, particularly in terms of evidencing your understanding of service user perspectives.

Activity 7.7: Supervision

Supervision is a fundamental building block of your placement. Reflect on the following questions:

- How do you evidence your learning about service user perspectives in written practice analyses, written reflections, and other work required for your portfolio?
- How do you explicitly refer to learning in supervision?
- How do you use extracts from your practice log?

By the end of your first placement you will have demonstrated your learning by meeting elements of the PCF. You will also have demonstrated competence in practice, and in your critical reflection on your practice. A good portfolio will demonstrate your journey of learning in the placement as you honestly and critically reflect on your own practice and how you have developed knowledge and skills to enable you to become a consciously competent practitioner at the first level (see Chapter 3). Therefore, your portfolio will be all the richer for your analyses on how you have learned, what has helped you learn, and who has helped you learn.

A service user perspective

As a service user representative, I am involved in the assessment of portfolios; and if I do not see the service user perspective integrated into the portfolio, I am very disappointed. It points to a lack of willingness on the student's part, and their view of the world. Sometimes I gain the impression that the student is there to rescue, but this should not be the case. It is about being there for the service user. Maybe in a small way.

There was an example of a student working with someone with hearing difficulties, and because they were aware of the service user's experience they made sure that they had set the room up appropriately and talked to other professionals about how they should speak to the service user so she could understand them.

I have noticed that students' values can be hit and miss. Some students challenge their placements and advocate strongly for service users. Their own life experience, and understanding the service user perspective, can help the student build their self-confidence enough to be an advocate.

I want to see humility – by that I mean the student stepping into the service user's shoes, but knowing they can't truly understand because they are not that person. Students need to appreciate the service user for who they are, and try not to be judgemental.

I want to see that the students are open to learning and having awareness. For example, you can have two service users in almost identical situations; but they are individuals, so they are not identical. Service users deal with things in different ways, and I want to see that students are aware of this.

Students need to see different perspectives. For example, mental ill health can have an impact in many different contexts. Students can develop tunnel vision, so they need to ensure they see the whole picture. There may be other professionals involved who do not understand the service user experience. Indeed, their family and friends may not – they may want them to be as they were. So it is important for the student to go in with an open mind and not let others cloud their judgement. I like to see how the student deals with these issues in their portfolio.

Review meetings

You will have read, in Chapter 4, that most programmes require a formal interim review and a final review of your practice placement. Reviews can be a celebration of learning, which will be all the richer for feedback from service users. Their feedback will be recorded and become part of your portfolio. Therefore, feedback from service users can become an important component to assess your progress and map your journey of learning towards being a qualified social worker.

An example of ground-breaking practice from a practice educator

At one agency, service users who misused substances had a graduation ceremony on completion of their programme. The practice educator was invited to the graduation ceremony arranged for the student at the end of the placement, where testimonials from service users and staff colleagues affirmed the student's values and abilities. This was an innovative example of service user feedback contributing to the final review and assessment processes.

Action planning

Having read this chapter, action planning in preparation for the placement could spark some great ideas. You could also use a session with your practice educator or placement supervisor to discuss involving service users meaningfully in your placement, and begin formulating an action plan.

Consider using a SMART model. This enables you to focus on being specific, ensuring that your goals are measurable, attainable, relevant and time-related.

Being specific

When you know where your placement will be, and the service user group you will be working with, you can begin your plan. Using examples from this chapter, devise some **specific** strategies on attaining service user involvement in your practice placement.

Is it measurable?

Will it benefit the service user/s? How do you think it will benefit the service user/s? How would you find out whether it was **measurable** for the service user/s?

Will you be able to relate what you want to achieve to your learning and the requirements of your course? Can you use the PCF to **measure** your attainment?

Is it attainable?

Having read the examples in the chapter, do you think you can involve service users in a meaningful way in your placement? How would you set about making involvement **attainable**? The PCF asks you to be creative – this is your chance to think creatively about the sort of involvement that might be possible.

Is service user involvement relevant to your learning and to the service user?

In your action plan you must clearly demonstrate the **relevance** of meaningful service user involvement to your learning. You must also reflect on the **relevance** to the service user. What is the benefit to them and to you?

Time-related

You have 70 days in practice in your first placement, and 100 days in your second placement. Reflect on what you can achieve in the time allowed, and plan accordingly.

SCIE (2009) recommended involving service users in learning and assessment as an essential component of good practice and a way of raising standards. Our programme subsequently set about devising strategies to enable students to involve service users in their practice education. We believe that this has led to a deeper breadth of learning for the student, and respect for the service user status.

On reading this chapter, we hope you feel as inspired as we have been and that you will make service user involvement a key element in your practice learning.

Key learning points

- Prior planning can enable service users to work in partnership with the student right through from induction to the final review of the placement. However, this will require commitment and support.
- Recognizing the value of service user involvement in practice education can lead to service users becoming part of the practice learning support team for the student on placement.
- It is possible to involve service users in direct observation of practice in a more meaningful way than simply asking consent when it is judged by all concerned as appropriate.
- Relevant feedback can also be acquired through the use of written forms.
- Acquiring a deep understanding of service user perspectives can facilitate professional development and enable you to meet the requirements of the PCF.

8 A continuum of lifelong learning

Lee-Ann Fenge

This chapter considers a continuum of lifelong learning, and looks forward to your future life as a qualified practitioner, including your transition to becoming a newly qualified social worker (NQSW) and your Assessed and Supported Year in Employment (ASYE). The chapter will also consider your future engagement with continuing professional development (CPD), and how learning through the portfolio of your qualifying degree sets out a template for future lifelong learning.

Lifelong learning is not only a desirable aspect of professional social work practice, but is an essential component of your future life as a social work practitioner. To respond to the continually changing context of social work practice it is important that you are able to engage in CPD, and become a competent lifelong learner. The portfolio of evidence that you develop through your degree in social work allows you to demonstrate longitudinal learning and progress across your placement learning experiences. Your portfolio also allows you to identify 'gaps' in knowledge that you may wish to develop further once you are qualified. The portfolio therefore allows the opportunity for retrospective reflection upon your learning and practice, as well as a prospective look forward to your future social work practice and skills (Taylor et al. 1999). This may relate to developing specialist knowledge concerning a particular service user group or setting.

A commitment to lifelong learning places a responsibility upon you as an individual to engage in CPD and skills development. This includes identifying your ongoing learning needs and the skills you will require to engage in the changing context of social work practice. The completion of a practice portfolio of evidence during your qualifying social work programme is a good grounding in identifying both your competence to practice and your ongoing learning needs. Once qualified, you will have the option of undertaking post-qualification training and education in your chosen specialist area of practice – for example, children and families, mental health, and adults and older people. It may be that the post-qualifying training and education you later follow will also require you to develop a portfolio of evidence to illustrate your learning, and you can directly draw on the experience of developing a portfolio of evidence from your qualifying training programme.

By the end of the chapter you will:

- Have reflected upon your own CPD needs
- Consider what AYSE means for you
- Be able to develop your own professional development plan (PDP), using your portfolio as a base.

Continuing professional development (CPD)

Continuing professional development is a key expectation throughout your social work career, and CPD continues to be a central plank of post-qualifying social work practice following the recent changes in the oversight of the social work profession. The General Social Care Council post-qualifying framework formally ceased its abolition in summer 2012, although higher education institutions can continue to offer post-qualifying programmes. A CPD framework was developed by The Social Work Reform Board, and this framework is now overseen by The College of Social Work.

As we have seen, the Social Work Reform Board identifies nine capabilities by which qualified social workers and students would be monitored and assessed (see the Appendix).

Building on the Professional Capabilities Framework (PCF) introduced in Chapter 2, you can see, in the Appendix, the nine capabilities that traverse both your learning as a social work student on placement, as well as your career development post-qualification. This includes your Assessed and Supported Year in Employment status, moving through to professional practice as a social worker, experienced social worker, advanced practitioner, and finally principal social worker.

Professional practice may be viewed as a period of personal and professional development prior to the advanced practitioner level. Advanced practice for the social care professions is about a level of practice well beyond initial qualification, and may embrace aspects of leadership and management, research and education; but it is firmly embedded in the delivery of good social work practice.

Advanced practice is founded on a depth of knowledge about the practitioner's practice, as well as an enhancement of skills of problem-solving and decision-making. Advanced-level practice may involve using complex reasoning, critical thinking, reflection and analysis to inform assessments, practice judgements, and decisions. These professionals may act as leaders in their field, managing their own workload and work across professional and organizational agency and system boundaries to improve services and develop practice.

Assessed and Supported Year in Employment (AYSE)

The ASYE replaces existing arrangements for newly qualified social workers from September 2012. It clearly links to the Professional Capabilities Framework, and therefore enables newly qualified social workers and their employers to develop a clear understanding of the appropriate skills and capabilities to be developed as part of CPD at different stages of their careers. It is expected that, once qualified, you complete the ASYE in 12 months. In a similar way that you may have completed a learning agreement as part of your practice learning and portfolio of evidence, you and your employer will also complete a learning agreement at the start of your ASYE period. This will include consideration of reflective supervision and workload.

A key part of this learning agreement will also consider your own personal development plan and protected time for personal development, which normally equates to 10 per cent over the course of the ASYE year. As you complete your portfolio of practice evidence, it may be useful to make of list of areas of practice, knowledge and skills which you may wish to develop further during your ASYE year for consideration in your personal development plan.

Activity 8.1: Reviewing portfolio evidence with regards to future CPD needs

PCF domain	CPD need
Professionalism	
Values and ethics	
Diversity	
Rights, justice and economic well-being	
Knowledge	
Critical reflection and analysis	
Intervention and skills	
Contexts and organizations	
Professional leadership	

A practice educator perspective

The Professional Capabilities Framework consists of nine domains providing opportunities for holistic assessment to be undertaken by practice educators at each stage of a qualifying programme. Each programme will have different requirements, but the process will always require regular consideration of evidence towards professional capability at the appropriate level. This process should occur at the meetings you have with your practice educator, and could involve reference to your written work as well as your actual work with service users and carers.

At the end of your practice learning placement, your practice educator will need to confirm that you are functioning at the level required by the PCF. This will vary according to whether it is a first or final placement.

You and your practice educator will identify areas of strength in your practice and any particular areas requiring ongoing CPD. It may be possible to identify specific domains, but more usually the continuing development identified will be in areas such as assessment or report writing.

Useful issues to consider when drawing up a professional development plan

When developing your professional development plan, it may be useful to consider findings from a study of newly qualified social workers by Bates et al. (2010) which suggested that a quarter of newly qualified social workers identified the following range of developmental needs:

- assessment
- report writing
- record keeping
- time management
- case management
- contracting.

Some of these areas may reflect specific local employer issues which can be bridged during the first qualified year in practice. For example, approaches to record keeping and report writing that are specific to the agency in which you work. You can consider these 'local issues' with your supervisor during your ASYE period. Alongside these specific local issues to practice, there may be other specific knowledge that has received less attention during your qualifying social work programme which you feel needs to be developed further. No matter how rigorous the qualifying degree programme, it is unrealistic to expect that it will prepare you for all aspects of professional social work practice. As Jack and Don-nellan (2010: 306) suggest: 'Qualifying training is probably best understood as an anchor for the development of full professional status during the early years of post-qualification experience.'

Research suggests that some specific areas of practice often receive little attention during qualifying education. For example, Galvani and Forrester (2011) suggest that substance use often receives very little input during qualifying education despite such groups being identified as one of the main groups of social work service users. They suggest that 'Many NQSWs do not feel prepared to deliver the types of assessment that the Department of Health and the National Treatment Agency suggest they should.' (Galvani and Forrester 2011: 435). Therefore, if you work in a setting where service users with substance use issues present, you may wish to develop your knowledge and expertise in this area.

The purpose of a professional development plan is to identify areas of strength and those requiring further development. Through developing your PDP, you are able to identify your specific learning goals and develop a structure for professional growth during your ASYE and beyond. When developing your PDP, it may be useful to consider the following:

- Developing a plan with your supervisor using learning needs identified within your portfolio as a starting point. Also consider the PCF, your own particular job role, and the goals of the agency in which you work.
- List goals and prioritize them. Will these be achieved during the ASYE period.
- Give headings to major personal development goals with specific plans of action and strategies of how these might be achieved during the ASYE period.
- Identify the resources and learning opportunities needed to achieve the goals, and the persons involved.
- Review the plan with your supervisor during your ASYE period. Redefine goals and plan of action.

Where do I want to be in a few years time?'

As you develop your PDP and review your CPD needs in light of your portfolio, you may also wish to consider what your longer term career aims are. Following the work of the Social Work Task Force, the National Joint Council for Local Government Services (NJC 2011) set up a working party to examine how the recruitment, retention and career progression of social workers might be improved. It is hoped that this will promote a consistent approach to career progression frameworks in England and Wales, with key levels running from newly qualified to advanced professional, team manager, practice educator. To support your career development, CPD should be based on the PCF and enable you to:

- demonstrate that they are maintaining and improving their skills
- extend and deepen specialist skills and knowledge
- acquire knowledge and understanding of, and contribute to, research which informs evidence-based practice
- develop as leaders and managers, both within their own organizations and within the social work profession
- become more confident, emotionally resilient, and adaptable to the changing demands of social work
- play an effective role in developing other social workers – e.g. as practice educators, mentors for NQSW.
- become the next generation of social work academics and researchers where appropriate.

(Social Work Reform Board 2010a: 33)

Pay scales and grading remain a local issue, and it is important to check with your employer how these levels are being used. However, by using the various levels described in the PCF and National Joint Council for Local Government Services proposals, it is clear that social work career progression for practitioners will span a number of levels:

- novice (ASYE/probationary) year
- social worker/licensed social worker.
- experienced/ senior licensed social worker.
- advanced practitioner, advanced professional, professional educator, social work manager.

As a newly qualified social worker, you may just want to concentrate on consolidating your professional practice before deciding on post-qualifying training. However, as you develop your PDP, it is useful to consider how your CPD needs might help you develop your future social work career. Although it is not a requirement for qualified workers to engage in a taught and certificated programme of study as part of their post-registration training, there are formal education options through the post-qualification framework which you may wish to consider.

There are post-qualification advanced awards at three academic levels – specialist, higher specialist and advanced. Five different areas of practice are covered:

- children and young people, their families and carers
- social work with adults
- mental health social work
- leadership and management
- practice education.

A practitioner perspective: (social work manager and professional doctorate student)

From my experience, continuing professional development not only develops professional competency but enables career progression. It relies on an ability to actively engage in career-long learning beyond simply accessing training. It requires practitioners to reflect on practice, their core values, agency expectations, and the skills and knowledge required in their role. Changes to the profession are regularly seen within our legislative framework, financial climate, or in the light of new research. It has been vital for me to engage with CPD to ensure up-to-date practice. I have been required to develop new ways of working, while ensuring existing knowledge continues to be fit for purpose.

I offer a brief reflection to illustrate the importance of CPD and how I used both formal training and informal support to develop my practice.

During the early stages of qualification, I sought to consolidate practical skills associated with:

- assessment writing
- formulating care plans
- producing funding requests
- writing case notes.

This illustrates how I found the transition from student to practitioner challenging. I felt pressured to adopt a practical mindset in favour of critical/analytical thinking. The pressure I felt to deliver on local authority targets and practical processes was considerable, and so clearly influenced the identification of my developmental needs. This gives credence to viewing CPD in more depth than just training. Colleagues suggested that the post-qualification framework might offer a way to better understand this tension. Post-qualification gave me the opportunity to reflect and critically explore best practice, along with other professionals. From this I gained better clarity of my role as a decision-maker. Recognizing the need for both the analytical and practical processes led to improved decision-making and independent thought. My development continued with the support of my manager, and helped to collaboratively set goals. We aimed to further develop my ability to independently make decisions which were ethically sound, and which were informed by my critical thinking. This also enabled me to deliver on local authority targets, but not necessarily be led by them. Together, we identified strengths and weakness in my practice, increased supervision time, and I accessed further training and engaged in peer support. As my skills and confidence grew, so did my level of practice and the complexity of my caseload. CPD and the post-qualification framework therefore enable me to:

- manage ethical dilemmas/ tensions
- have confidence to apply critical thinking to all cases
- work as an autonomous professional
- balance local authority targets with social work best practice

- set aside time to plan strategically
- deliver creative services which are person-centred
- make ethically sound decisions
- deliver informed, well-reasoned assessments.

By recognizing the need to continually develop I have been able to consolidate and increase my skills and knowledge. This has developed my level of professional autonomy, ethical decision-making and problem-solving, enabling me to optimize the life opportunities of the service users I support, and develop my own career.

I now hold a management position. This has taken my development full circle as I once again have to balance a different set of local authority targets and practical processes against my own practice. However, by actively engaging in my own CPD, I have the awareness, internal resources and skills to better manage such tensions.

Concluding points

- Always have CPD as an agenda item on supervision records.
- Use supervision to highlight any tensions/issues.
- Identify strengths and weakness regularly.
- Make a plan with your supervisor to develop your practice.
- Use both formal support from supervisor as well as informal peer support.
- Consider CPD to be more than just training.

The College of Social Work and CPD

The College of Social Work seeks to support CPD for all levels of social work by:

- promoting organizational and personal responsibility for CPD
- providing support to maintain core HCPC re-registration standards
- encouraging knowledge and skills development to the higher level set by the PCF.

You will therefore work in partnership with your employers to identify your future CPD needs.

Key learning points

- Your portfolio is a vital building block for your social work career; it provides you with evidence of your strengths and ongoing learning needs, and a range of transferable skills.
- Lifelong learning is not only a desirable aspect of professional social work practice, but is an essential component of your future life as a social work practitioner.

- A PDP is central to your CPD, and is a way to identify areas of strength and those areas requiring further development. Your PDP allows you to identify your specific learning goals, and develop a structure for professional growth during your ASYE.

The portfolio provides a springboard for your lifelong learning journey; use it to prospectively look forward to your future social work practice, and the types of CPD you may wish to engage with.

Useful links

The College of Social Work: http://www.collegeofsocialwork.org/newly-qualified-social-workers/

Skills for Care: http://www.skillsforcare.org.uk/Home.aspx
Health and Care Professions Council: http://www.hpc-uk.org
For adult sector enquiries, email: ASYE@skillsforcare.org.uk
For children's sector enquiries, email: ASYE.SG@education.gsi.gov.uk

Appendix

Professional Capabilities Framework for Social Workers

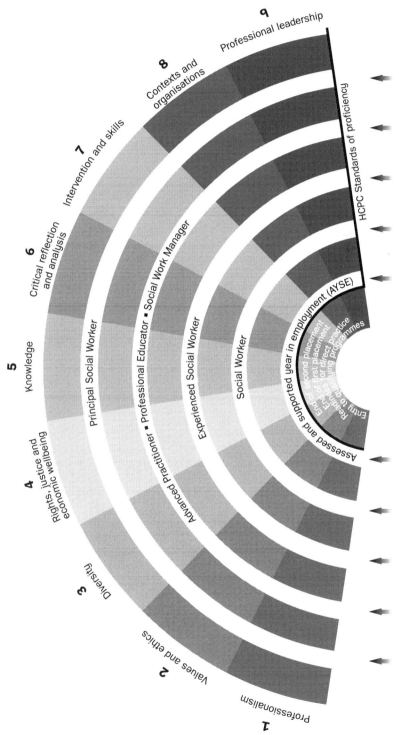

1 Professionalism
2 Values and ethics
3 Diversity
4 Rights, justice and economic wellbeing
5 Knowledge
6 Critical reflection and analysis
7 Intervention and skills
8 Contexts and organisations
9 Professional leadership

Principal Social Worker
Advanced Practitioner ■ Professional Educator ■ Social Work Manager
Experienced Social Worker
Social Worker
Assessed and supported year in employment (AYSE)

End of second placement
End of first placement
Readiness for direct practice
Entry to qualifying programmes

HCPC Standards of proficiency

References

Alvarez, A.R. and Moxley, D.P. (2004) The student portfolio in social work education, *Journal of Teaching in Social Work*, 24(1/2): 87–103.

Bates, N., Immins, T., Parker, J., Keen, S., Rutter, L., Brown, K. and Zsigo, S. (2010) 'Baptism of fire': The first year in the life of a newly qualified social worker, *Social Work Education*, 29(2): 152–70.

Boud, D. and Miller, N. (1996) *Working with Experience: Animated Learning*. London: Routledge.

Boud, D., and Walker, D. (1998) Promoting reflection in professional courses: The challenge of context, *Studies in Higher Education*, 23(2): 191–206.

Bourdieu, P. (1984) *Distinction: A Social Critique of the Judgement of Taste*. London: Routledge.

Branfield, F. (2007) *Shaping our Lives: User Involvement in Social Work Education*. Swindon: Acorn Press.

Branfield, F. (2009) *Developing User Involvement in Social Work Education*. London: SCIE .

Byrne, M., Schroeter, K., Carter, S. and Mower, J. (2009) The professional portfolio: An evidence based assessment method, *The Journal of Continuing Education in Nursing*, 40(12): 545–52.

Chapman, A. (2010) *Johari Window*, available at http://www.businessballs.com/johariwindowmodel.htm [Accessed 28th May 2012].

Chapman, A. (2012) *Conscious Competence Learning Model*, available at http://www.businessballs.com/consciouscompetencelearningmodel.htm [Accessed 28 May 2012].

Chow, A.Y.M., Lam, D.O.B., Leung, G.S.M., Wong, D.F.K., and Chan, B.F.P. (2011) Promoting reflexivity among social work students: The development and evaluation of a programme, *Social Work Education*, 30(2): 141–56.

Coleman, H., Rogers, G. and King, J. (2002) Using portfolios to stimulate critical thinking in social work education, *Social Work Education*, 21(5): 583–95.

The College of Social Work (2012a) *Accessing the PCF*, available at http://www.tcsw.org.uk/pcf.aspx [Accessed 28 May 2012].

The College of Social Work (TCSW) (2012b) *Professional Capabilities Framework*, available at http://www.tcsw.org.uk/ProfessionalCapabilitiesFramework/ [Accessed 18 December 2013].

The College of Social Work (TCSW) (2012c) *Understanding what the different levels mean*, available at http://www.tcsw.org.uk/uploadedFiles/PCFNOVUnderstanding-different-PCF-levels.pdf [Accessed 20 December 2013].

Collingwood, P., Emond, R. and Woodward, R. (2008) The theory circle: A tool for learning and for practice, *Social Work Education*, 27(1): 70–83.

Covey, S. (2004) *The 7 Habits of Highly Effective People*. London: Simon and Schuster.

Crisp, B.R. and Maidment, J. (2009) Swapping roles or swapping desks? When experienced practitioners become students on placement, *Learning in Health and Social Care*, 8(3): 165–74.

Davys, A. and Beddoe, L. (2010) *A Guide for the Helping Professions*. London: Jessica Kingsley Publishers.

Dundon, K. (2012) *Reflective practice in child protection*, available at http://www.socialworker.com/home/Feature_Articles/Professional_Development_%26_Advancement/Reflective_Practice_in_Child_Protection%3A_A_Practice_Perspective/ [Accessed 10 July 2012].

Fenge, L. (2008) Realising potential? The challenges of widening participation for students, further education and higher education. Unpublished DProf Thesis, Bournemouth University.

Fenge, L. (2011) 'A second chance at learning but it's not quite higher education': Experience of a foundation degree, *Journal of Further and Higher Education*, 35(3): 375–90.

Fox, R. (2004) Field instruction and the mature student, *Journal of Teaching in Social Work*, 24(3–4): 113–29.

Galvani, S. and Forrester, D. (2011) How well prepared are newly qualified social workers for working with substance use issues? Findings from a national survey in England, *Social Work Education*, 30(4): 422–39.

Gardner, H. (1996) Probing more deeply into the theory of multiple intelligences, *NASSP Bulletin*, 80(583): 1–7.

Gee, J.P. (2001) A sociocultural perspective on literacy development, in S.B. Neuman and D.K. Dickson (eds) *Handbook of Early Literacy Research*. New York: Guildhall, 30–42.

Gibbs, G. (1998) *A Guide to Teaching and Learning Methods*. Oxford: Further Education Unit, Oxford Polytechnic.

Graham, G. and Megarry, B. (2005) The social care work portfolio: An aid to integrated learning and reflection in social care training, *Social Work Education*, 24(7): 769–80.

Greenwood, J. (1998) The role of reflection in single and double loop learning, *Journal of Advanced Nursing*, 27(5): 1048–53.

Harrison, K. and Ruch, G. (2007) Social work and the use of self: On becoming and being a social worker, in Mark Lymbery and Karen Postle (eds) *Social Work: A Companion to Learning*. London: Sage, 40–50.

Hawkins, P. and Shohet, R. (2006) *Supervision in the Helping Professions*. Maidenhead: Open University Press.

HCPC (2012) *Standards of Proficiency – Social Workers in England*, available at http://www.hpc-uk. org/apply/socialworkers/standards/ [Accessed 26 September 12].

Holliway, D. (2009) Towards a sense-making pedagogy: Writing activities in an undergraduate learning theories course, *International Journal of Teaching and Learning in Higher Education*, 20(3): 447–61.

Honey, P. and Mumford, A. (1986) *The Manual of Learning Styles*. Maidenhead: Ardingly House.

Hughes, M. (2011a) Do challenges to students' beliefs, values and behaviour within social work education have an impact on their sense of well-being?, *Social Work Education*, 30(6): 686–99.

Hughes, M. (2011b) Unitary appreciative inquiry (UAI): A new approach for researching social work education and practice, *The British Journal of Social Work*, Advanced access available from: http://bjsw.oxfordjournals.org/content/early/2011/10/19/bjsw.bcr139.full [Accessed 13 December 2013].

Hughes, M. (2012) The impact of social work education on the whole person. Unpublished Thesis (Doctorate in Professional Practice), Bournemouth University.

Jack, G. and Donnellan, H. (2010) Recognising the person within the developing professional: Tracking early careers of newly qualified child care social workers in three local authorities in England, *Social Work Education*, 29(3): 305–18.

Kadushin, A. (1976) *Supervision in Social Work*. New York: Columbia University Press.

Kolb, D.A. (1984) *Experiential Learning: Experience as the Source of Learning and Development*. London: Tavistock.

Kolb, D.A. (1999) *Learning Styles Inventory*, version 3. Boston: Hay Group.

Kolb, J.J. and Funk, J. (2002) Kolb's learning style inventory: Issues of reliability and validity, *Research on Social Work Practice*, 12(2): 293–308.

Lake, F. (Undated), cited in Waskett, D.A. (1995) Chairing the Child – A Seat of Bereavement, in S.C. Smith and M. Pennells (eds) *Interventions with Bereaved Children*. London: Jessica Kingsley Publications, 45–67.

Lam, C.M., Wong, H. and Leung, T.T.F. (2007) An unfinished reflexive journey: Social work students' reflection on their placement experiences, *British Journal of Social Work*, 37(1): 91–207.

Lee, M.Y. and Greene, G.J. (2003) A teaching framework for transformative multicultural social work education, *Journal of Ethnic and Cultural Diversity in Social Work*, 12(3): 1–28.

Mackay, K. and Woodward, R. (2010) Exploring the place of values in the new social work degree in Scotland, *Social Work Education*, 29(6): 633–45.

Mackenzie Davey, K. and Arnold, J. (2000) A multi-method study of accounts of personal change by graduates starting work: Self-ratings, categories and women's discourses, *Journal of Occupational and Organisational Psychology*, 73(4): 461–86.

Mezirow, J. (1996) Contemporary paradigms of learning, *Adult Education Quarterly*, 46(3): 158–72.

Mezirow, J (1997) Transformative learning: Theory to practice, *New Directions for Adult and Continuing Education*, 1997(74): 5–12.

Mezirow, J. (2003) *Epistemology of Transformative Learning* (PDF), available at http://184.182.233.150/rid=1LW06CB3L-1R1W965-1Z5Z/Copy%20of%20Mezirow_EpistemologyTLC.pdf [Accessed 10 January 2013].

Mezirow, J. and Associates (1990) *Fostering Critical Reflection in Adulthood*. San Francisco: Jossey-Bass.

Milner, J. and O'Byrne, P. (2002) *Assessment in Social Work Practice*, 2nd edition. Basingstoke: Palgrave Macmillan.

Morrison, T. (2001) *Staff Supervision in Social Care: Making a Real Difference for Staff and Service Users*. Brighton: Pavilion.

Munro, E. (2011) *The Munro Review of Child Protection: Final Report: A Child-Centred System*, available at https://www.education.gov.uk/publications/eOrderingDownload/Cm%208062.pdf [Accessed 31st May 2011].

The National Joint Council for Local Government Services Working Party on Recruitment, Retention and Career Progression of Social Workers (2011) *Recruitment, Retention and Career Progression of Social Workers: Final Report*. London: LGA. 2011.

O'Sullivan, E. and Taylor, M. (2004) *Learning Toward an Ecological Consciousness: Selected Transformative Practices*. New York and Basingstoke: Palgrave Macmillan.

Race, P. (2007) *The Lecturer's Toolkit: A Practical Guide to Assessment, Learning and Teaching*, 3rd edition. Abingdon: Routledge.

Reupert, A. (2007) Social worker's use of self, *Clinical Social Work Journal*, 35(2): 107–16.

Sadd, J. (2009) First substantive placement 70 days, *Bournemouth University Social Work Practice Learning Handbook*. Bournemouth: Bournemouth University.

Sadd, J. (2011) '*We are more than our story': Service User and Carer Participation in Social Work Education*, SCIE Report 42. London: SCIE.

Schon, D. (1987) *Educating the Reflective Practitioner: Towards a new design for teaching and learning in the professions*. San Francisco: Jossey-Bass.

Schon, D. (1996) *Educating the Reflective Practitioner: Towards a New Design for Teaching and Learning in Professions*. San Francisco: Jossey-Bass.

Sims, S.J. and Sims, R.R. (eds) (1995) *The Importance of Learning Styles: Understanding the Implications for Learning, Course Design, and Evaluation*. Westport, CT: Greenwood Press.

Skills for Care (2002) *Statement of Expectations from Those who Use Services and Carers*, available at http://www.niscc.info/content/uploads/downloads/workforce_dev/nos_health_social/statement_expectations.pdf [Accessed 10 January 2013].

Social Work Reform Board (SWRB) (2010a) *Building a Safe and Confident Future: One Year On: Detailed Proposals from the Social Work Reform Board*, available at https://www.education.gov.uk/publications/eOrderingDownload/1%20Building%20a%20safe%20and%20confident%20future%20-%20One%20year%20on%20-%20detailed%20proposals.pdf [Accessed 31 May 2011].

Social Work Reform Board (SWRB) (2010b) *Building a Safe and Confident Future: One Year On: Progress Report from the Social Work Reform Board*. London: Department of Education.

Social Work Reform Board (SWRB) (2010c) *Practice Educator Professional Standards in Social Work*, available from http://www.tcsw.org.uk/uploadedFiles/TheCollege/_CollegeLibrary/Reform_resources/Practice-EducatorProfessional(edref11).pdf [Accessed 10 January 2013].

Social Work Task Force (2009) *Building a Safe, Confident Future: The Final Report of the Social Work Task Force*, available at http://webarchive.nationalarchives.gov.uk/20130401151715/https://www.education.gov.uk/publications/standard/publicationdetail/page1/DCSF-01114-2009 [Accessed 10 January 2013].

Swigonski, M., Ward, K., Mama, R., Rodgers, J. and Belicose, R. (2006) An agenda for the future: Student portfolios in social work education, *Social Work Education*, 25(8): 812–23.

Taylor, I., Thomas, J. and Sage, H. (1999) Portfolios for learning and assessment: laying the foundations for continuing professional development, *Social Work Education*, 18(2): 147–61.

Timmins, F. (2008) *Making Sense of Portfolios*. Maidenhead: Open University Press.

Walker, J., Crawford, K. and Parker, J. (2008) *Practice Education in Social Work: A Handbook for Practice Teachers, Assessor and Educators*. Exeter: Learning Matters.

Walmsley, A., Thomas, R. and Jameson, S. (2006) Surprise and sense making: undergraduate placement experiences in SMEs, *Education and Training*, 48(5): 360–72.

Wenger, E. (1998) *Communities of Practice: Learning, Meaning and Identity*. Cambridge: Cambridge University Press.

Williams, S. and Rutter, L. (2010) *The Practice Educator's Handbook*. Exeter: Learning Matters Ltd.

Wilson, K., Ruch, G., Lymery, M. and Cooper, M. (2008) *Social Work: An Introduction to Contemporary Practice*. Essex: Pearson Education.

York Model of Observation (2011) Department of Social Policy and Social Work, University of York.

Index

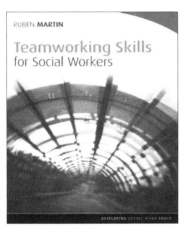

TEAMWORKING SKILLS FOR SOCIAL WORKERS

Ruben Martin

9780335246052 (Paperback)
2013

eBook also available

Social workers are members of teams and need to work in collaboration with colleagues and other professionals in order to practice effectively.
This book explores the dynamics present when people work together, the roles individuals play and the skills necessary for effective teamworking in the context of social work practice.

It provides a practical and applied overview of the different types of teams social workers encounter.

Key features:

- Specific links to the new Professional Capabilities Framework for Social Workers
- Checklists to help the reader rate their capability and plan ways of developing skills for which they score low
- Reflection points

www.openup.co.uk

**AN INTRODUCTION TO APPLYING SOCIAL
WORK THEORIES AND METHODS**

Second   Edition

Barbra Teater

9780335247639 (Paperback)
April 2014

eBook also available

This bestselling book is the leading introduction to the
most commonly used theories and methods in social work
practice. Now in its second edition, the book explores the
concepts of a 'theory' and a 'method', the difference
between the two and the ways in which they are connected.
Assuming little to no prior knowledge, each chapter
explores a single theory or method in depth and uses a
variety of interactive tools to encourage the reader to
explore their own theories and beliefs.

Key features:

- New chapter on **Community Work** provides a step-by-step
  approach to community work
- New chapter on **Groupwork** provides an overview of the
  rationale for groupwork
- New **case studies** exploring areas of growing priority
  in practice such as dementia

www.openup.co.uk
||||| OPEN UNIVERSITY PRESS
McGraw - Hill Education

CONTEMPORARY SOCIAL WORK PRACTICE
A Handbook for Students

Barbra Teater

9780335246038 (Paperback)
February 2014

eBook also available

This exciting new book provides an overview of fifteen
different contemporary social work practice settings,
spanning across the statutory, voluntary, private and third
sectors. It serves as the perfect introduction to the
various roles social workers can have and the numerous
places they can work, equipping students with the
knowledge, skills and values required to work in areas
ranging from mental health to fostering and adoption, and
from alcohol and drug treatment services to youth
offending.

Key features:

- An overview of the setting, including the role of the
  social worker, how service users gain access to the
  service and key issues, definitions or terms specific
  to the setting
- Legislation and policy guidance related to the
  specific setting
- The key theories and methods related to the setting

www.openup.co.uk

DAVID **WILKINS** & GODFRED **BOAHEN**

Critical Analysis Skills
for Social Workers

CRITICAL ANALYSIS SKILLS FOR SOCIAL WORKERS

David Wilkins and Godfred Boahen

9780335246496 (Paperback)
2013

eBook also available

Analysis is a critical skill for social workers, yet it is
a skill that many practitioners find very difficult. This
book will help social workers to improve their analysis
skills by offering a very basic, step-by-step model to
develop an analytical mindset. It shows how analysis can be
woven into the whole process of social work engagement,
resulting in better decision making, more efficient ways of
working and, ultimately, better outcomes for social work
service users.

Key features:

- What analysis is, and why it is such an important
  skill in practice
- The skills that underpin critical analysis, e.g. time
  management, planning, critical understanding, logical
  thinking, research-mindedness, creativity,
  communication, reflection and hypothesising
- The role of emotion and intuition in critical analysis

www.openup.co.uk

OPEN UNIVERSITY PRESS
McGraw - Hill Education

15729209R00081

Printed in Great Britain
by Amazon